T0160751

SEVEN
YEARS
TO
ZERO

SEVEN YEARS TO ZERO

AMY BENSON

DZANC
BOOKS

DZANC
BOOKS

5220 Dexter Ann Arbor Rd.
Ann Arbor, MI 48103
www.dzancbooks.org

First US edition: May 2017

Book design by Steven Seighman
Cover and interior art by Katie Shima

Dzanc Books thanks Rhodes University for their support of this project.

ISBN: 978-1-941088-77-7

Library of Congress Cataloging-in-Publication Data

Names: Benson, Amy, author.
Title: Seven years to zero / Amy Benson.
Description: First edition. | Ann Arbor, MI : Dzanc Books, 2017.
Identifiers: LCCN 2016038922 (print) | LCCN 2016044196 (ebook) | ISBN
  9781941088777 (softcover) | ISBN 9781945814105 ()
Subjects: | BISAC: BIOGRAPHY & AUTOBIOGRAPHY / Literary. | GSAFD:
  Autobiographical fiction.
Classification: LCC PS3602.E6852 A6 2017 (print) | LCC PS3602.
E6852 (ebook) |
  DDC 813/.6--dc23
LC record available at https://lccn.loc.gov/2016038922
Printed in the United States of America

10   9   8   7   6   5   4   3   2   1

For Beals, who brought them

CONTENTS

FORWARD

We come from towns where the water runs thick with nitrogen in the spring. Or towns where front lawns are covered in white stones and defensive plants. Towns where we know the kid they're collecting for at the gas station. Towns in which the most crowded buildings are nursing homes. Towns where a girl disappears and you will find no one who saw it coming.

We come from suburbs with churches the size of malls. Suburbs where they fix Brazilian cocktails and cleaning fluid drugs. Suburbs where the houses are squat bunkers and the trees cool and tall. And suburbs where the doors and walls are hollow.

We come from cities that have worked their rivers brown. Cities with the scars of streetcars. Cities that buy their movie reviews from the newspapers of other cities. Cities that like dogs and scrapped-tire decking and wild-caught salmon.

We come from places where people get close enough to touch only across cashier counters. Where you might believe you are the first to see something, own something, bury something.

We thought we didn't have accents or style. We thought we'd been uncreased. We thought polls were never talking about us. And we've come to the tallest, densest place, a city that will never need a marketing campaign. But we come with our eyes normal-sized and open in our heads.

In fact, we didn't always want to come, and we worried, some of us, about what might happen to our brains: how could we think when we knew that in every direction, for miles, millions of people were also thinking. The air looked like a nest of wires.

We visited a city beach once, before we moved, but we could not get into the ocean, though it was ninety degrees, though we love the water. A few feet was the farthest we could have gotten from the next pair of legs. Everyone the same water, the same sand. How could we imagine our thoughts were new?

These thoughts, we suspect, will come less and less frequently. We are a demographic, and there will only be more of us—a map littered with pins, all threads leading here. At the threshold of the hive, we almost never feel like we're in a prison of lungs and legs and greasy palms. We're happy with an open park bench.

YEAR 1

The apartment's previous occupant died here. We painted each room of our new home a vibrant citrus color. From the subway platform, we could see our office glowing chartreuse. We thought, Oh, who lives there—we do! Look at us from a distance! We ripped out the corroded kitchen and laid a new floor—substrate and then blue clay tiles that reminded us of the Italian countryside neither of us had visited. We thought, We are people who can build a floor. And then the tiles buckled and cracked, the building too uneven and the tiles too large for the four-by-nine room; by now we are used to the way they crunch slightly under our feet.

We learned that, more than a century before, a public well stood a few feet from our building. People brought jugs and basins to gather clean spring water, unavailable in other parts of the city. It flowed to a nearby dairy and to a brewery, which was later shuttered during Prohibition. They were forced to dump 840,000 gallons of beer into the gutters that led to the river at the end of the road. We learned that we are one block south of a flood plane, a fact we did not think would be useful. That was a few years before we saw the blue lines *artists painted around the city to mark projected sea levels, before the hundred-year flood, to be known henceforth as the forty, twenty, the ten-year flood.*

In the meantime, we visited a gallery show with three simple pieces:

1) *The ends of a length of wire poked through the wall in two places. We looked once and hardly noticed, then looked again and saw that the wire was moving. In fact, it was in constant motion—protruding from one hole while retracting through the other, then back again. Slow, steady movement. We watched until we grew dizzy, thinking we might be the ones in motion, swaying toward and away from the wall, following the moving wire into the wall and back out again.*

2) *A smooth black ribbon stretched from ceiling to floor, winking and shifting as if it, too, were moving. We inched closer and closer. A thin stream of black liquid—oil? yes, oil—poured from a hole in the ceiling into a hole in the floor. The line thinned and swelled minutely, shifting in unseen air currents. Occasionally the stream seemed to reverse direction and travel up into the ceiling. But this must have been a trick of the light, yes?*

3) *A sizeable section of floor was covered in weathered asphalt—it might have been lifted from any aging street. In the center, a circle had been cut in the asphalt and it was slowly spinning in place. This is not what asphalt was meant to do. We leaned toward the circle as if toward a vortex.*

The show transitioned seamlessly to the street, and on the way home we were unsteady on our feet, wondering what section of concrete might begin to spin, which grate was a trap door, which doorway tromp l'oeil.

Where we came from, people talked about "nature" without quotation marks, as if it was real and obdurate and they were in it. We used to say nature, when we were where we came from; but now, a long way from home, we were glad to live in a city with magic tricks. Where we might not always trust our eyes or feet—rather, where our eyes might lead us into a story we could not have conceived. It made optimism easier.

THE OCTAGON ROOM

It looked like a temporary shelter preparing for deluge. That is what we saw when we walked into the gallery—a little structure built from unadorned plywood, buttressed by two-by-fours, and shored up with sandbags. There was the suggestion that, despite the reinforcements, one jostled beam and the whole thing might fall open like a blown flower. When we stepped inside the room, however, we were in the implacable nineteenth century, stranger to compressed wood and polypropylene bags.

It was, in fact, an octagon room, fad of the mid-to-late 1800s for people who liked a wall so much they wanted a new one every time they shifted. In the middle of this octagon room was an octagon settee, one wedge of dusky rose upholstery facing each wall. Sit, it said, and study. And there was much to study. Part genteel office, part Wunderkammer, part natural history museum, the room was a fistful of lists. Maps, antique desks, drawings of fish and birds, excavation tools, specimen jars, card catalogue bureaus. Taxidermied animals; shards of pottery dredged from riverbeds; bookshelves with Spencer, Conrad, Machiavelli; and notes and sketches, some of which appeared to represent a nascent version of the room itself. Every item hinted at a history, a field of study, a way of framing the question, as if, 150 years ago, a net had been dragged through the northern European forests, rivers, libraries, and museums, the bounty hauled home and painstakingly organized.

The imagined proprietor of the room was a gentleman scientist, natural historian, collector, archaeologist, environmentalist, humanist, and colonialist. A Victorian intellectual who wrote a book for every idea he had, easy in his anticipation of mastery.

But the artist who created him was wise about that desire to label and preserve, about the assumption that collecting equals knowing. And he had a wicked sense of humor. There was a shadow box lined with labeled keys, the handsome script on which suggested some keys might open real gates or doors or boxes, and some might open imaginary museums or even portals to other worlds. Deer heads mounted on the wall looked as if they'd been fished from the Exxon Valdez spill. A map was hung so high above the doorframe that it became entirely unable to inform or direct.

After a while, we zeroed in on a favorite: a taxidermied turtle. It was posed as if in mid-step, and piled high on its back was a conglomeration of shell, stone, sand, and human artifacts—

teacup shards, buttons, fragments of antiquated children's games. As if it had hibernated for several centuries in the mud and, at last, risen up through the layers, its shell an archaeological dig. Turtle was, breath by labored breath, hauling it all into the future.

If we could have taken the turtle home, we would have. A reminder of the weight of human history crawling across our coffee table. Our guests might focus on the turtle's front foot poised to step and politely ignore that it was stuffed by the very same instinct for preservation that says: I'll kill you, but I won't let you go.

We stayed as long as we could, itching to thumb through the card catalogue and contents of the roll-top desk. We had the strong impression that the room was telling us something essential, something we needed to know before we could move on. We had come in from the street, where we were learning selective sensing—how could we notice every noise, every threat, follow the news feeds scrolling 360 degrees around us, and still get where we were going? We had grown up learning how solutions became problems and order became greater chaos—how cats brought in to catch mice themselves needed catching; how spent nuclear rods piled up in the no-longer-cool cooling baths; how a war to end all wars scattered the seeds of a thousand more; how there was something in the water no matter the well. Now here were eight walls of sincere collection and its brilliant critique. We thought we might be able to absorb the Octagon Room's *modus operandi*. See everything, including the limitations of our sight.

We stayed until our attention became strained, a performance, and then slipped outside and looked back. We were shocked to see, once more, the plywood, the sandbags, shocked at how, inside the room, we would have disavowed any memory of the raw and flimsy present. It was a blow but not a surprise to learn from a gallery attendant that the show would close in another week. The room would go into boxes, and then...where?

Before the week was up, we returned with a digital camera and, without considering the irony, photographed every inch of all eight walls—180 pictures, at which we have never looked back.

CLAW INSIDE THE SKULL

A squirrel cage is for pest removal. Inveigled within, the squirrel does not stop moving, inside its chest a hummingbird heart. Claws, rimmed with tiny squirrel diseases, stick through the mesh here and then there. It loops, it lunges caddy-corner. The squirrel has turned itself into a cartoon. Maybe it will be shot or drowned or taken far from the easy food and released.

"Squirrel cage" also describes a mental trap. An animal circling in the mind. The same thought threatening but never burning out its heart. One's father might say, "I'm in my squirrel cage," and one might wonder how a man who drew straight lines for a living had gotten so comfortable with metaphor.

We recently wanted to create a mechanism for offloading these mental animals, and we came up with a cluster of cylinders that spin, like hamster wheels or Bingo tumblers, but made of cherry-stained wood, the sides cut through with intricate carvings. The carvings are based on patterns in photographs—fossil impressions, seed pods, a wolf print in sand, the branches of a newly constructed grape arbor— and the photos were taken in the wilderness where one of our fathers lives as a hermit much of the year. There is an excess of beauty in this place, but the father's mind can only allow for the reverse image: how he might one day lose everything he has. He sets traps for mice and red squirrels, which are terrible, he says, just terrible. He sits inside without a view and considers his ruins.

We often think of this place when we are not there, but these thoughts are not problematic.

The cylinders of the mechanism are attached to columns and the columns are attached to a sturdy base, to one another through gears and pulleys, and to a handle on the side. Turn the handle and seven lovely cages spin.

The sculpture, entitled "Distributed Squirrel Cage for Parallel Processing," recently spent some time in the company of other pieces that moved or spoke, projected or displayed. An art exhibit might come down to this: it either extracts something from you or it slips something inside. One calls the former *catharsis* or *a waste of my time*; one may not find the word for the latter. Distributed Squirrel Cage for Parallel Processing offered visitors the opportunity to write an obsessive thought on a piece of paper, ball it up, press it through the slats of the cage, and turn the handle. Goodbye thought. Hello bicep. Hello to the conditions of your release. Your ratty thought tumbling with the thoughts of strangers.

———

Today an envelope from the museum came in the mail, flat-rate and bulging. Somehow the envelope became open and inside were hundreds of scraps of paper. In their history as paper, first they were trees, then logs, pulp, pressed paper, then crumpled, then smoothed so they looked like the palm of a hand unfurled. Obsessive thoughts given over to the squirrel cages and now released onto the living room floor.

Was the museum allowed to do this? Perhaps they should have considered an incineration clause.

Do I smell? Can somebody smell me?

That story I read in the *Denver Post* fifteen years ago about Bosnian rape camps.

Someday I'll leave and he won't recover.

Cells dividing. Maybe in my lungs. Brain? Maybe down in the colon. I've had too many toxins in my life.

Fuck you.

The idea that my toes can shoot bullets and I have to curl them to keep from hitting anyone.

I'm never going to make something as good as "The Nesting Dolls" again.

I can't protect them.

There might be poison in my food. And also, is there a diagnosis for me.

Oceans rising

My career is finished. I'm finished.

Those T-shirts I brought back from Florida—will the kids like them?

They took everything and they want me to keep smiling.

Not smart enough.

I'm doing the same crap my mother did and Marlo's going to hate me.

About everything bad I've done. Can't list it all here.

Something getting mixed in with the recycling and ruining a whole batch.

Why did I say that Why did I say that Why did I say that I can't stand to be inside my flesh.

Money

dirty bombs

Earthquake. Falling way, way down in a crevice. And what's it like down there.

Is it too soon? And: how many have I had?

Teeth falling out.

The potion I made in a dream once and can't remember the ingredients. It was going to change everything.

Dad or Mom is going to get Alzheimer's. Probably Mom.

One lock is not enough.

I've wasted so much of my life. And it's not like that's going to change.

Spent nuclear reactor rods

Nobody listens

I touched one door jam when I came in but not the other, and I can't go back to touch the other because Sarah is standing right here.

They were extracted and now they have been slipped inside.

THE LAST ROOM

Humans learn occlusion on their way out of infancy—the ability to grasp that the toy still exists when it's under the blanket. Blanket does not extend through the bed to the floor, floor does not extend to the center of the earth. There is a behindness, an other side. We learn there's a yard beyond the bedroom wall; sinew under the skin; and eventually, we're told that beyond the atmosphere, which looks to our eyes a flat and toothless blue, there is a solar system, and, beyond that, more systems in every direction.

We haven't lost things when we can't see them. Neither are we safe because danger is out of sight. We follow the rules of matter even if we can't discern them. This is the world of the human adult. There is something behind everything. Yet we hardly relax into this knowledge; to manage the unseen, humans often require worry beads, religions, equations, drugs.

Then one day we walk into a room. We thought we were walking into a gallery, and at first we fear we've made a mistake, taken a wrong turn; that somehow, between the door and the briefest of hallways, we've lost our way, wandered into an empty storeroom. Or perhaps the door was meant to be locked, a gut renovation as yet unfinished.

We are embarrassed to ask the lint-free gallery attendants, and so we pause, let the room sink in. Imagine walls thicker than you can imagine, made of white plaster, then put the room in a desiccator. The plaster is half on the walls and half on the floor—cracking, sliding, chunking to the ground. We can't see the motion, but we can feel the infinitesimal entropy at work.

Rubble heaps on the bare floor. Fissures at least a foot deep scar the plaster on the wall. The room's nearest kin is a glacier—clefts in a behemoth, calving to the slushy sea below.

But the room has none of a glacier's history. Blue ice pummels and drags every age with it, deposits anachronism as it goes. This space is pure white but looks like a ruin. Not in our generation was it made, and yet it has no patina. It is a physical conundrum: timeless and immediately ruined. The last room on Earth to be discovered. We must have missed the headline: ON REMOTE DIG, ARCHAEOLOGISTS FIND INFINITY. A piece near the ceiling flakes and clinks to the floor. A bit of dust, an echo, then the room is as it was.

What time is it? Has the room closed for the night? Is the plaster lit or lighting the room? Perhaps we're moving at the same rate as the walls. The longer we're in the room, the more certain we become that we've misapprehended the rules of matter—occlusion does not hold. Behind the wall is simply more wall. It will continue to fissure and slough and fall away. The room will slowly fill with rubble. There will be no more room for eyes. We study the room as if our lives depend on it. A blink and then we're gone.

We have been doing this thing with our minds for so long—traveling to real but invisible places. We know, for example, that there is an apartment next door with a neighbor in it, though we never see inside and rarely hear him. Sometimes there is a vibration through the shared wall, though we can't say what it is. We picture him, with his rice cooker and still-life puzzles.

We leave the only room, travel home again through timed lights, on sidewalks over trains and sewage, and find ourselves standing next to our neighbor, fumbling our keys, nervous because an intimate stranger who may know things about us is trying as desperately as we are to get in, to get safe. Surely we know he has not disappeared when he shuts the door behind him, though it may seem that he has, though it may seem that we have. Nothing beyond our walls but more wall.

FLASH

There was one piece in the show we hadn't seen yet. We watched other visitors enter a hallway and then, after some time, exit looking scooped out and mirthful. We wanted part of whatever cul-de-sac they'd paused in. The hallway zigzagged and was painted black so as to outrun all ambient light, and at the end we entered—was it our ears that told us?—a fully dark room also painted black. Dark as in not a shard through the iris, not the narrowest pipette.

We couldn't tell what—or who—might be in the room. In the absolute dark, you lose track of the habitual pose of your face. You lose "plan" and "then." You merge with the air, and whatever you hold in the creases of your palms flutters down. Perhaps five seconds went by before a bright white light flashed. In the flash we saw there was nothing in the room except for other visitors, who looked, in the pop of light, caught out at something, revealed. That millisecond of light seared an image of the room onto our retinas and persisted, though our eyes were wide open and drying in the dark. Ten seconds later, another flash of light, another tableau burned into the brain. Ten seconds after that, another.

Afterward we thought, *It put the light inside us in a way that it always is.* It's easy to forget this, easy to think that we are watching the world around us, not watching reflected light inside our own heads.

For the next ten seconds, this micro-slice of time was what the brain thought was true. As with a camera in low light, the flash created an image, and the open shutter of our eyes preserved it. We had time to study the room in our heads: a man in a track jacket bent as if in strong wind; a couple joined at the fingers, shoes creeping forward; a teen-age girl still and straight, thin arms pinned to her stomach, mouth and eyes repeating circles.

Even if we chose to stand perfectly still, others could have moved. So there was no escape from the knowledge that light brings. Time passes; an image from ten seconds ago is ten seconds old. The knowledge that what was burned into the brain, what was our mind's *only* truth, could be entirely replaced ten seconds later. The girl is gone, the couple parted.

It was good fun—a small explosion in the eye, the brain, the adrenal gland. We stood perfectly still at first, paralyzed by the discrepancy between what our eyes told us and what the room might actually hold. And then we gasped and thrilled at the strands of flight in our hands, and we dared the light gathered in our minds—played a heart-stopping game of tag, ran into people, found ourselves inches from a hairy arm with the next pop of light, forgot that the darkness had not also taken our voices, then found our way out, hands trailing along the hallway, found our friends and laughed ourselves sideways.

We did not know then that we would go home and tap our foreheads in the dark of the bedroom that was not now dark enough. The things we'd seen, the things we see now, now, now are already gone.

RIBCAGE

If a cow and a deer got into a stupidity contest, it's unclear who would win, and what they would win. Still, to a deer, a wall can be had. Humans seem perpetually surprised by what's stored in the haunches of a deer. A cow will pretend a wall isn't there, but that involves strict and obsequious observation of the wall. The cow can't recall the content of its legs.

When an artist decides to make a fence or an outdoor wall, you can be sure that the effort is not to keep in or keep out. He or she will make a wall about walls. It might be fashioned from inappropriate material, such as hair, cardboard, or a conglomerate of recyclables. Or the wall might be made of plaster and then eaten by the artist. The wall might have embedded messages about border conflicts. It might be trained to move when the viewer least expects it. A rule of thumb: in art, there must always be surprise. An artist could build a wall into the side of a hill so that it disappears unless you seek it out, run your fingers across its many names.

———

There is a wall in a well-acred sculpture park bordering the far end of the property. First you view primary-color steelworks that could only have been created by a crane and a mind that does not believe in miracles. Though this mind does not mind appearing miraculous. Then a sculpture that looks as if it's survived a burn, wood so dark and scarred it seems to have become conscious. It makes you think of dead industries, the holds of slave ships, mineshafts, textile factories that went up with one spark in the cotton-dust air.

Another piece you walk on before you know it's art.

Beyond these many pieces, at the border of the woods, is the wall. It is made of ordinary masonry, the kind of wall one might find between fields, keeping domestic animals from one another. But it doesn't do what a wall should do, because it's a wall about walls. It trails in and out of the tree line; though solid, it moves like a brook. Occasionally, it ceases to exist—the mind perceives the absence while the eye finds the missing stones and taps them into place.

In the sculpture park, visitors are not encouraged to walk into the surrounding woods. At dusk, the deer, who require no invitation, sample the grasses in the hill troughs, sometimes climb to the peaks on spindly ankles. They look like lawn ornaments. They compose a photograph that would be classified as either ironic or "nature," pretty and possibly sentimental.

———

Nightfall, when the deer leak through the gaps in the wall, drop by drop, you drain the other way, into the woods. Quickly you lose light. There was so much deliberation on the other side; here there is none, though there is surprise: a spider's web across the face, tree bark turning into moths, a small hill vibrating with ants. Through the night you hear sounds that reference other sounds.

And in the morning, where are the deer? Not in the fields, though you can see the swirls they've made in the grass here and there, like cowlicks on a fine head of hair. Their ribcages are larger than you can fit your arms around. But there are other means of observation. You could ask a hunter for the carcass, dry the bones, flesh stinking no longer than you'd expect. You could make a cage of deer ribs with plaster or resin or wood and place something unexpected inside: headlines of war arranged in collage; a leafy houseplant tucked into an artificial tree trunk, the vines of which trail down the spine to the ground; a video screen the size of a heart that loops footage of deer springing through a field.

You can see the towering steel sculpture in the distance—a bright yellow architect's remnant, a physics lesson painted *caution*. You have things to do. Your Toyota pickup is on the opposite side of the park. But your feet are sandbags. You can't cross the stone wall, even where it is no longer a wall, only a suggestion of a wall.

If there were a video screen where your heart should be, what would it loop?

A CLEAR CUT

We are trying to piece together the order of perception. We can agree that the windows were frosted and we saw nothing before we entered the gallery. We walked in and we exhaled, and kept exhaling, down to the air that rarely stirs from the lower lobes. The hairs on our heads settled, our brains relaxed into their cranial baths, something warm trickled down our spines. Our mouths, which had been poised, fell slack.

We think we felt those things first, before we registered the scent of cedar that filled the gallery. And we think the scent came before we noticed that the far back wall of the gallery, a single cavernous room, was covered floor to ceiling in smooth cedar planks. Our eyes said the room was empty, but the caves behind our noses, under the skin of our cheeks, knew it was thick with cedar scent molecules. We walked into the room, molting electrical energy.

Then we noticed on the side farthest from the door a corroded claw-foot tub filled partway with water. Did we see the actual bath before we thought of our brains bathing?

It's possible. It seems most of the time, we don't know what we know. After a moment, a slight clanging alerted us to the two tubes draped over the side of the tub, which connected to a coffeemaker sitting on the floor, clear water in its glass carafe. Water flowing from the coffeemaker into the tub shook and lifted one of the tubes. The other tube presumably sucked water from the tub to the coffeemaker.

The hot front part of our brains wanted to churn into it: why a coffeemaker, why a bathtub, is this foolish? But something, not a thought but adjacent to it, sifted over us: the coffeemaker was a heart. A simple circulatory system— kitchen counter, rustic bathroom. Mug of black coffee, end-of-day body. Some of us stuck a finger in that water, but we weren't sure what we wanted to learn.

The longer we stood in the room, the more we began to think of the artist and how she arrived at this empty, occupied space. We still felt extraordinarily calm, but we realized it was not the calm of absence but of excision. She had begun with many ideas, decades' worth, many mistakes, with rolls of unused chicken wire, with uncertain relationships, rehearsals of old arguments, diagrams, elaborate fantasies, fragments of memories and dreams, with tubes and plaster, paint and bricks. She wanted to be everything, have everything, use everything. But her stubborn, haunted will cut and cut until she had just the two, three things she needed. She made a clear and simple room, the aftermath of a controlled burn, teeming with ghosts.

One is supposed to leave after a while. Our senses dull; as happy as a show has made us, we grow restless. On the floor by the door sat a stack of posters and a sign that said TAKE ONE. The poster featured the artist's name—Virginia, of course—and a blown-up photograph of a chain tied around a cedar trunk and the muddy tracks of an off-camera truck pulling the felled tree from a bog. Another photograph appeared on the show's flyer: four stumps, a thick spray of sawdust, and the sagging pants of a man, a chainsaw on the ground by his boots. The flyer said that the wood, the tub, and the coffeemaker were taken from the Tennessee farm on which she'd grown up.

She had this whole room, she could have put anything in it. She went back to her past and cut it down. She dragged it out of the swamp. She shipped it, planed it, sanded it, and nailed it to the wall.

What an enormous racket we made in the woods, when we were young, a thousand miles away from this place. An obliterating smell.
The textures we left behind were mostly jagged.
Chainsaw, wood splitter, truck and trailer.
Pulled up to our brick bunker and laid in the winter's wood.
Flecked with sap, smelling of gasoline, sawdust fluffing our hair.
We were nature people.

We could take it apart because we loved it. And no one else loved it as we did.
The language of a lover and abuser are sometimes indistinguishable:
I love you, I know you,
you're mine.

We took the old jeep deep into the forest, fought with the primitive paths.
There were always chains in the jeep, a saw,
and holes in the floor so big we might have lost our legs.
And a rifle and a lamp.
We'd train them on deer in the night, stop them in their tracks.

Virginia, we think we know you; we were there, where we owned things roughly and they owned us. And now we're here, where things are ideas and we move in a colloidal suspension. We are all a long way from home. The boards are smooth, the scent is strong, we are calm and clear. We'll take a poster, tape it above our bed, but we don't want to leave.

Out the window, around the corner is the chain we dragged behind us, snagging four states' worth of debris.

YEAR 2

It could have been one year, could have been three or four. We dissolved, we amalgamated, we became part of the city. A helicopter could not have distinguished our heat from the heat of others—we were lava flowing through the streets, underground, up through the tubes of buildings. Our movements were recorded a hundred times a day. We sometimes shared a wave with the conductor when the elevated train stopped across from our apartment, but we noticed the screeching breaks only in their absence—quiet meant disaster. The surface of the sidewalk came home with us every evening: ginkgo berry, shoe bottoms, dog nails, the grit that fell like a fine mist daily, matter extracted from human lungs, stomachs, bowels, bladders, and the somatic cells of at least six other species. We made soup.

We lived in the middle of perpetual construction—new buildings, new art. We made things, then we held onto clammy subway poles and went to see what others had made—a room full of oil and twinkling lights, giant bears made of cardboard and eggshells drenched in honey-glue, a statue of a man bound by two chains; the links of one chain were iterations of his index finger, the other, his tongue. We stuffed our eyes full every day. When we crawled into our bedroom and closed them, often the images did not quiet. And the lights that glowed through the night penetrated the thin skin of our eyelids. Oven, microwave, laptop, cell phone, modem, humidifier, power strip, streetlight, emergency exit, planes in flight overhead. We tried to count the lights just in our apartment but we repeatedly lost track. Having no way to close our ears, we heard the way the neighborhood kept itself humming through the night.

Sometimes we had to leave the city. We used the Internet and a GPS to find swimming holes in the forest, pools carved out by rivers. We stripped naked on the rocks and jumped in, shrieked with glee into an empty forest. We bought little boats that folded up into bags and dropped them into every body of water we could reach. We went to the wilderness where one of us grew up and foraged in the woods and in the ditches at the side of the road. We thought, out there, of the art that we had seen—children with abnormally sized genitals, animals suspended in resin, pornographic battle scenes fashioned from toys. In the city we thought of an otter we met once when we'd paddled well past the last human shelter; we fashioned an acrylic icon of her and hung it from our rearview mirror.

All that we saw and heard and touched fluttered down like shredded newspaper and compost. We lay down on it and took a long nap.

WATER SHELTER FOOD AND FORM

A shipping container is virtually indestructible, built to preserve the perishable or unstructured on a journey to places where the contents will be consumed, crushed, incorporated, or dissolved. The container will not.

On a hilltop in the Jura Mountains, in the middle of grazing fields and plowing fields, thirty empty shipping containers were delivered and arranged in an irregular circle, some filling in the middle and some stacked one atop the other, a few set sideways, bridging lower-level containers. A crane was used, there were many people in hard hats, a few with clipboards. Those with clipboards had the pleasure of seeing a sketch become three-dimensional steel and the worry that someone might literally be crushed for that pleasure.

The Jura Mountains are growing: yet-to-be-eroded stone buds are solid proof for geologists that what used to be ocean floor is rising. The shipping containers feel as if they have either dropped from a disconcerting future or pushed up from the secretive past—a *Mad Max* version of Stonehenge. On the treeless hilltop, a place to run to or from.

In a day or two, people will climb the hill with boxes and cases, wires, speakers, and tool kits and occupy the containers. A week after that, visitors will come to see what they've made.

Hikers piss in caves and leave their snack wrappers; caves seem now, in other words, a place to hide bodily functions. Early humans may have used caves for safety, gathering, ritual, and seasonal sleeping. Prehistoric human rubbish heaps found outside caves throughout the Jura hold hazelnuts, marmot and red deer bones, intentionally chipped stone. The stone was sometimes chipped for more than tools or weapons, as caves in the Jura have given up ivory carvings of mammoth, manlion, and horse, line and expression visible still. Caves like those at Pech Merle, Lascaux, and Chauvet were painted with color that would last nearly thirty thousand years and counting. Art today requires climate control, insurance, restoration, or it is deliberately transitory. Artists surround eleven islands with floating fabric for fourteen days or create outdoor murals with paper and wheat paste.

One of the mysteries of art is that it seems to have dropped into the human mind fully formed. The figurines and the cave paintings are stunningly graceful. If humans evolved an aesthetic ability, where are our fumbling early attempts, the toddler drawings, the mess of etchings on rocks? Of course, discoveries were made along the way: perspective, abstract subjects, conceptual art, the idea that one might call anything art and naming it makes it so. But thirty-three thousand years ago, humans already knew about occlusion, hiding animals in stomachs, behind rocks. And they knew about depicting expression and movement. The mammoth is all light and control; it is about to break into a canter. It may be one of the first instances in which form did not first answer to function.

The people who will build pieces into the shipping containers are housed with volunteers in nearby villages. We are hosted by a middle-aged Swiss couple in a tiny village a fifteen-minute walk away, past a cow field and an orchard. It is not surprising that the house was extraordinarily neat. A few days into the weeklong stay, the Swiss man's mother will die. We will not know what to say or how to make ourselves smaller.

During the day, we sit on the hilltop in the now-bustling shipping container village and fasten fishing line to a thousand wooden blocks and hang them from the ceiling of our allotted container. We will build a wooden drop ceiling and fix each fishing line to it with a staple gun. Each time like the report of a rifle—a thousand blasts across the hills.

In the end, though, it's a delicate piece, nearly silent. Blow on the trigger and the agitators in the center knock a few blocks, which knock their neighbors, the blocks rippling toward and away from you as if a stone had been tossed in a still pond. Your breath made visible, and then subsiding.

Elsewhere, people are installing a light organ or fastening robotic mallets of every sort to the inside of a container, coaxing a percussive orchestra out of the steel walls, or setting up an interactive game with stackable tiles that, when added to the board, change the pitch and frequency of the projected sound. On the ceiling of one container is projected footage taken from the undercarriage of a big rig in motion. Speakers broadcast the heaving machinery of the truck—rush of air, whir of rubber on tarmac, tiny pebbles spitting up and glancing off the camera. When the viewers enter, they are asked to lie back on the floor as the doors close behind them; and when the doors reopen, they stagger out clutching their heads or stomachs.

At night, past the slug-filled cow field and orchard, we tiptoe up the stairs, the rest of the house dark. But the man is likely not asleep. Strangers on the stair, his mother in the ground. The easiest thing to say is that art cannot help him.

We are filling our storage containers not so many kilometers from the home of a well-known maker of spectacles. A tinkerer on a large and small scale, interested in chains of reaction, in simultaneity, in using the castoffs of industry and entertainment to create yet more industry and entertainment, he once built an enormous, animate rubbish pile meant to put on a show and then self-destruct. It produced drawings, colored smoke, and layers of sound, but it did not destroy itself. A train ride away, through a valley known for a now largely defunct watch industry, there is a museum devoted to preserving the tinkerer's work. Push a button and the machines will creak and move for you, old from the day they were born.

The evening of the festival, visitors are, indeed, festive, arriving by train and bus and carload from cities and the villages in between. Ladies in fluttering dresses, men in colorful socks. It is a lark, a happening—here they are, on a hilltop in the middle of nowhere!

Many things await at the top. Electronic instruments wrangled by a Belgian family, the patriarch of which prefers to perform nude but conceded to be clothed on this night. An elderly Frenchman in clogs conducts a washing machine orchestra. Dancers wearing wings and amplified sirens climb the hill like valkyrie, moving through the containers, scaling them, broadcasting what—music or alarm? They broadcast alertness. It's a call to something, though no one can say what.

An hour or so into the evening, an answer comes in the approach of black and sparking clouds. Soft bodies, altitude, metal—danger nearly as old as the hill itself. The people with clipboards herd others down the hill to a welcome tent. The rain falls purple and thick, cut to ragged strips by lightning, for longer than they could have imagined. When it is finished, the ground oozes mud; it engulfs the shoes of the visitors and they go home.

The next day, in a now-misting rain, clouds on their heads, the artists and crew and people with clipboards will break it down. Wood scraps into crates, electronics into rolling suitcases, instruments into padded boxes, a bin for everything that cannot be salvaged. In a few years, the field will heal.

But for now, this night, after the visitors have left, the people who have made this thing slog back up to the empty, alien village and turn on the light organ again. The elderly Frenchman who conducted the washing machine orchestra brings out a fiddle. People stomp and twirl in ankle-deep mud. Flecks fly up to their faces and hair.

The music is not recorded as evidence or culture. It is a muscle twitching. The installation needs this joy and this privacy, just as the fiddle and folk dance need the installation, the small crowd of virtual strangers with warehouse minds and twelve languages, the cows, the faded industrial valley, and mountains full of caves, hazelnuts, marmot bones, and inscrutable secrets.

The thirty-thousand-year-old mammoth in motion, the crate of wooden blocks for burning. It is always, always this: a moment in the the context of forever.

TEN YEARS AGO THEY WERE ALL SO YOUNG

She first came on the scene at the Presentation—five foot one, angel-faced, with chocolates for everyone. Individually wrapped in cellophane, the chocolates were like craggy planets or futuristic golf balls. Some attendees had them out of the packaging and into their mouths before she opened hers. A few sunk a tooth in to see if there was something (or nothing) inside. Others were more circumspect, holding it up for a closer look—was it chocolate or art? It was more and more difficult to answer questions like that.

"What you hold in your hand is a representation in chocolate of a virus that threatens human lives. This virus is invisible to us, and scary. And maybe it's scary partly because it's invisible." She went on to tell them what the virus did, how many people were infected, and how many people might become infected in a difficult-to-imagine future. People collect such projections: in 2015, one in one hundred will be homeless; in 2040, fresh water will be more precious than oil; in 2050, we will have to abandon our coastal dwellings.

She said she had taken electron microscope images of the virus and stolen time with a 3-D printer at work when she should have been creating a client portfolio. With the printer she fabricated molds of the virus, and in her kitchen filled them with chocolate—the good kind, she said with a smile, though she didn't elaborate. At first the chocolate was a vehicle, but soon she became absorbed in the choc-olatiering—the smoothest taste, the glossiest finish. "This is the fifth-generation model." A hint of pride passed over her lips.

She said she had grown to love the shape of the virus; she could see it behind her eyelids. She did not say she was sick. In fact, she looked radiant. Everyone thought about her face, which might bloat or pock or jaundice with the disease or its medicine.

Those who had eaten the chocolate immediately now looked a little unsettled at their gluttony. Or was that queasiness at having unwittingly popped back a virus?

A few held their chocolates from a cellophane corner, left it on the counter near the exit as they left. Perhaps they were imagining her kitchen—she *had* invited them to imagine her kitchen—a tiny cut on her hand, the relative cleanliness of the sponge.

Many, though, took the virus out, held it up, turned it around, felt it softening in their fingers. Though she had not said what she wanted, they gingerly tasted the virus, then took it in as something sweet.

She resurfaced a year later at the Museum's annual artists-under-thirty exhibit. Everyone was there to break their hearts on who was or was not on the walls or the floor or hanging from the ceiling. She was none of those things. They found her on the great lawn, which sloped steeply from the museum's back terrace. She had her viruses with her again, only this time she was standing next to them and they rose several feet above her. They were composed of an interior aluminum structure covered by an inflatable outer layer, dimpled and ridged just like the virus. It was a giant, bumpy beach ball you could climb inside. The free-swinging seat in the center kept the passenger upright, even as the ball rolled down the hill.

The visual was lost on no one: shunting downhill, gathering speed, engulfed by the virus. Still, there was a line behind the beaming artist. She helped them inside the next virus and gave them a slight nudge. And for ten seconds, they had the time of their lives.

DEAD LETTER OFFICE

We went to see a gallery show called "Dead Letter Office" because we'd heard there was a man in a Plexiglas box. What we saw upon entry was not as kink as that might suggest. The box was the size of a very large room and there were several tables and a desk scattered with art supplies—piles of patterned paper, fabric, paints, dried vegetation, books of what looked to be photos of Japanese vases, primitive tools, renderings of the Pieta. It was, in short, a workshop.

He was seated on the floor, making tiny cuts into paper he held close to his face. Remnants of a sandwich sat on a plate next to him like a still life awaiting a title. He did not look up; he didn't even appear to be trying not to look up, perhaps because it was the third week of a four-week show. An elegant bed occupied a far corner—four posters with drapes he might pull around himself, we supposed, for a nap.

The program said the artist had studied the Greeks, had studied world religions (and here we began to itch—another artist trying to be more than what he's placed on the wall or floor), and found they had one thing in common: transubstantiation. In our most important stories, over millennia, one thing turns into another. Water into wine, rock into river, awe into envy, dust into lungs and hearts and skin, gods into animals, maidens into laurel, into salt, into wind, children into pigs and stone, everything into birds. So why is it that inside us, he wondered, sifted down to the bottom of every organ, are these hard and persistent lumps—regrets, angers, thwarted hopes—like briquettes that won't light, stones that refuse to pass? The human story of the world is mercury and lava. But the human *in* the world is weighted and bagging.

Had we ever been to a Dead Letter Office? the program asked. He had—no, that was a lie, but he had thought about them a lot. (And here we returned to him with affection. We liked to be deceived and then confessed to in rapid succession.) Piles of undeliverable letters—words that would never become birds and then land and become something else.

Now he got to the point: what we were looking at in the box was his attempt at transubstantiation. *You are invited to write down something you have never been able to say to someone, something that has sat like a stone inside you for years—your own dead letter—and include an address to which it might be sent. He will read your letter and then create an artwork on a postcard. On the back he will simply sign, "Love, (your name)."* He would live in the gallery for a month and work and eat and sleep and mess up, start again, grow frustrated, stare at the ceiling, perhaps entertain visitors, likely groom himself in inappropriate ways—a scratch, a pick. He would be a live conduit, an elf, transmogrification made flesh. Leave a stone, your addressee will get a seed. Follow the metaphors, let them become one thing and then something else.

We wondered what it might smell like inside the box after three weeks.

We had read somewhere that the average museum-goer spends thirty seconds in front of a painting and sixty seconds in front of a film or video. We watched him for a good ten minutes while he cut paper. Snip snip snip. Filigreed shapes emerged. He reached for the paste. But we didn't know if anything had changed for the depositor—or would change for the recipient. Despite his glass house, we could not see a fairy tale, and we realized we were waiting to catch him in some little bodily drama, as if we were spying through a neighbor's window. Everything he did was quite regular, and we simply didn't have that kind of time. There were ice cream cones to eat, books that needed to be picked up and then set back down.

We moved on to the wall where he had tacked the letters (with the names blacked out) already completed—more than a hundred. Most began generically: "I know it's been a long time" or "I've always wanted to say this but never found a way," and we stopped after a dozen or so. Not because they were unoriginal, but because they were too familiar, each stranger's aged drama falling a long way inside us and sticking. Oh this mother and son, oh this wounded friendship, these serrated loves. Who needed more of the same?

Oh Medea, oh St. Peter, oh Delilah with your hands full of hair.

On the way out, we paused at the table with paper and pens, and, though we harbored a host of regrets and unsaid monologues, each one a tragedy the size of the tiniest matryoshka doll, we did not write a letter.

At home we imagined discussing with one another why we left no letter. Maybe because this was an artwork and we wanted to *view* it, not *be* it. And what of the work of art he would send? Perhaps the recipient would find it trite or graphic or an unwanted provocation. We simply didn't have the energy to play along—all that writing, all those feelings. Probably, we were afraid. Probably, our stones were ballast and we didn't want to float away.

We found the program to the show a year or so later in a towering pile on the desk. We smiled, then, at his optimism (and a bit at his hubris—the Greeks, indeed!), but we didn't let ourselves regret our choice or imagine the postcard that might have arrived into a silent and dimly lit berth. We put the paper into the recycling pile, but even days later the program rankled, the physicality of it. Surely there were stacks of these sheets somewhere still—in the gallery's back office, in his portfolio, his mother's attic. Paper, like the postcards, that will weight someone's desk, until it's hauled away, chewed up, and pressed into something new: tissue box, toilet roll, letter paper.

FAIRYTALE CITY

The girl with the tiny voice was a surprise. She stopped us on the street, said, Would you like to yell something?

Did we look angry?

You don't have to be angry to need to yell. She said this so sweetly it was practically birdsong.

Did we have time for this? Was there a catch? Even birdsong could trap and bedevil.

She held up a furry blue bag the size of a large purse and shaped like splayed lungs. We could have called it a creature if we'd been feeling affectionate. There was an opening at the top, dark-lined, leading to its belly.

You see, she said, and took a giant breath. She bent over, mouth to opening, and turned squint-eyed and red in the face, the smallest cottony sound leaking out the sides. Then she stepped to the curb, leaned over the street, and squeezed the bag. Something that started as a rumble and soared into a battle cry fell out. We fought to get our hands on the creature.

The first one of us gave the kind of generic whoop you might hear ricocheting from a canyon. The second put some lung into it, and there were banshees in her lungs. We looked at her in surprise. The third spent a long time with the creature. The words she used must have been down in a low place for a long time. They came up muddy and mossy, through a great deal of effort. She watched serenely as the girl with the tiny voice knelt low under a tree and emptied the sound onto the grass. We tried not to listen, but there was something about five years and water and never. The last one, we don't know and he isn't saying. The girl walked away with his yell under her arm.

The next time we saw her, she was on a screen. A little video festival in a theater that was trying to be less blow-shit-up and more funny-pants. We were already tiring of videos; we wanted to see risk right in front of us. But we went.

Until the moment she appeared, we thought perhaps we had hallucinated the scream incident—like so many moments that take up residence in an alternate city in our minds. The tiny ancient cowboy, for example, walking down our quiet neighborhood street with a belt buckle the size of a dinner plate.

But there she was, eye level with a blender. Sweet-faced and pixie-haired and growling. The blender growled back, low, a little test of its voice. They looked at each other—that's the way it seemed—surprised and pleased. She regrouped and came back with a melodic howl; the blender ramped up to a whir. The girl growled and howled, like a charming animal. The blender responded

in kind, a stately elder finding his tucked-away exuber-
ance. She stopped, looked away. The blender cleared its
throat. She started, looked, blinked. It revved again. She
smiled. The end.

After, there were drinks and then some harsh words
among us. Harsh words that came from bad feelings and
led to more bad feelings. The feelings and words got stowed
again at the end of the night, though we knew they might
mildew. It is difficult in this city to remember to go back
through static, to label and discard it.

All night, in our beds, we could hear the refrigerator,
the overloaded power strip, the digital clock all murmuring
through the dark, and we didn't know what to say.

Not long after, we were at a low-key little gathering—a
friend of a friend lucky enough to have a patio. The first
heat of the summer was coming on and we were eating
meat on sticks and starting to sweat through our clothes.
She came in with a bag, kissed the host on the cheek, and
wandered the periphery of the patio, greeting people who
took her hands, brushed her hair behind her ears, clearly
loved her.

We trailed her shamelessly, though we couldn't hear
what they were saying, her voice was so small. "Hey, what
happened to my scream?" one of us wanted to ask, but he
did not want to sound cute. In truth, we only wanted to
listen.

Late, when the group had thinned—and we should have
thinned with it, given how well we didn't know our host—
he prodded the girl, Come on, let's see it.

No, it's not ready.

But she relented and produced from her bag a white orb, which she placed in the lap of the host. It was like a giant egg, the size of a pregnant belly. He sat with his hands on it and his face slackened, his eyes closed. We kept sending words out of our mouths to strangers seated near us and tried not to stare as the egg made its way around the circle.

Finally, it came to us. It was covered in what felt like very high-end doll skin—pliable but firm, ever so slightly powdery. As it sat there, an inch away from our organs, it began to breathe. Not a robo-ventilator tube breath, but an erratic infant breath, the kind you hang on, that you try to breathe with your own lungs to make sure they keep going. It moved just as delicately, expanding and shifting. We spread our hands, trying to take more of it in. Our blood moved to the surface of our skin as if to greet it.

Perhaps it was the meat in our bellies, the fact that smells had just that week come rushing back with the spring heat, that our skin was exposed with the scant cut of our clothes, but we could not deny our parts, our animal parts. Except for our eyes, which we closed to move more fully into our selves and into the egg, which hardly now seemed separate.

We held onto the egg too long, overstayed our welcome, but we did not want to open our eyes.

It was like that, seeing her three times, a fairy tale number, and we expected she might be part of our lives now—she and her things that turned around inside of us and purged the wrong things and allowed the right things to fall in place, like a key in a tumbler. Click. But we never saw her again.

We miss her. We miss her so much. In our minds, we each hold a white room with three objects: blender, furry bag, and egg. We wonder, will the egg stay alive long enough for someone to pick it up and decide he should not set it down again?

THREE SHEEP

They ordered the sheep before they knew what they would do with them. Three. It seemed like the right number. When they arrived, in the back of a metal slat truck, the couple realized the choice had limited their options. Sheep came inscribed with storybook barnyard motifs—red barn, split-rail fence, water troughs, a meandering driveway under a great big sky. Between bites of grass, the sheep looked up at them like lost pieces in a child's play set. There were factory defects, of course. One of the sheep had a crusty eye, a fly stuck to its cheek and another circling for what could only be an unpleasant meal. The woman thought it probably needed some ointment. The man wondered, what sort of ointments did sheep use?

It was the beginning of not knowing a lot of things. In the past, they never knew what they were doing, but then one of them would make a move—order supplies, throw out a title, streak a few lines on a piece of paper—and a path would assemble itself before them, like a hologram.

Other people always seemed eager to see what had materialized.

Several years earlier, an empty milk carton lingered on the kitchen counter, joined shortly by another and suddenly they announced themselves as the building blocks for a walled city, the buildings inside which would be made of Starbucks cups, cereal boxes, tofu containers. Eventually, wine bottles sprouting crushed wrapping paper shaded streets paved with the gold-striped interiors of French fry cartons and hamburger wrappers. Canals rippled with spent take-out foil. Electrical wire floss (subtly spotted with blood), straws, cork, endless corn chip bags—all turned, in dollhouse proportions, into a city that called to mind the future, one's lunch, and a medieval past.

Assistants built viewing platforms with coin-operated, behemoth binoculars, like the ones that fringe Niagara Falls.

Visitors were invited to use their own food packaging to add outlying developments—sprawl accumulating through napkins, juice boxes, cellophane, water bottles. The silver insides of energy bar wrappers made excellent roofs and roadways.

They knew the press would come in bulk. Critics were allowed to speak knowingly about consumerism, uncontained expansion, the new imperialism, the city filled with stuff yet empty of people.

Still, the project wasn't cynical. The walled city was intricate. They added detail even where no one might look—substrata of Styrofoam and bubble wrap under the roads, broken glass mosaic on the cathedral floor, visible only from a difficult angle. The piece rewarded further study.

They became very intimate with their own trash, saved it for a year—the virtuous, organic, grass-fed milk cartons, and the damning: Tastykake wrappers, countless fry cartons (they didn't realize how many until they were collecting in a bin). Take the Tastykake wrapper: they had to face, months later, the bit of chocolate frosting smeared on the inside, the memory of the sweet emptiness.

They were canny, not calculating.

Which was why they ordered the sheep. They figured once the sheep arrived, with their heaving wooliness and cloven feet, they'd see the line and follow it to the end. But this time, it didn't happen.

Perhaps they should have ordered alpacas, somehow wilder-seeming and yet enjoying a wave of popularity. Or pigs, which come with the irony of human revulsion and yet genetic proximity. But pigs dig, and the man had heard they were disconcertingly smart.

They sat on the front stoop and watched the animals have their way with the grass, the hostas, the decorative sweet potato vines and kale.

As night fell, they knew they had to get the sheep from their miniature and now closely cropped front yard to the slightly larger back lawn. They tacked cardboard and sheets across the doorways to adjacent rooms, creating a long, straight chute from the front to the back door. The sheep trotted through, their spindles a blur.

When that grass was gone, they bought family-sized bags of oatmeal from the Stop-n-Shop. The sheep ate the oats for a while, without gusto, and soon turned back to the grass, which they brutalized. With delicate, nearly obscene quivers of their lips, they found the nubs of grass and guillotined them at the dirt.

For the first week or so, their minds worked almost audibly, scratching for an idea. Instead of using the sheep in a show, they could shear them and make a piece from their wool (maybe a network of the kinky hairs pulled apart to create a wall—transparent but impassable). Or they could branch into other media: record and photograph the sheep in their now-natural environment, put them online—v-logs and p-logs. But it all folded flat in the mind.

What they needed was a plan. Instead, a temporary imperative stuttered out.

Most of the front yards on their block in Queens were tiled or poured with concrete, often with matching concrete shrines to Mary or a saint they couldn't name. A few blocks over, though, the shrines thinned out and the yards got larger, lusher. No one liked to mow. A few more blocks and there were grassy medians, parks. They would offer their sheep, themselves, to their neighbors. Move at dawn and dusk—would sheep wear collars and leashes?—and evade detection and whatever statute they must be breaking against farm animals in the boroughs. Could this be considered performance art? With no commission and no audience and no idea tucked into the folds of the action? No, they were no novelty act. They were just feeding their sheep. Not even *their* sheep, just sheep.

———

Their days narrowed to this: watching the sheep unhook and rotate their jaws endlessly. She held a stick to keep them away from the owner's roses or kitchen herb garden or ivy trellises. She had wrapped a Christmas sock around the end so as not to hurt the sheep when she prodded. The sheep didn't look at her as a sheep might look at a shepherd, she thought.

The curious thing was their eyes—meaty, blue-white, with reptilian slits. They had never seen an eye they could so easily imagine as a meal.

The curious thing was the top of their legs, where the wool ended and the hair began, cloud into stick. You could see through the skin, there, to the thin bone below.

The curious thing was their tails, fuzzy stumps that wagged when they ate, like a dog's. It was difficult not to ascribe to the tails dog-like emotions—happiness, excitement, devotion. This could not be the case. There was nothing but sky behind their meaty eyes.

The curious thing was the teeth, which looked a great deal like his departed grandmother's. She had lived to a great age and had literally become long in the tooth—her teeth stretched and yellow and increasingly independent of one another. Their furred lips pulled back and he thought: crocheted toilet paper cozy, brandy in rosehip tea. He didn't think: installation, bold but nuanced gesture.

The curious thing was the way they moved in relation to one another. They grazed, seemingly aimless, until one picked up its head and trotted with great energy, its stub of a tail clamped over its privates. The other two would flank it immediately, and they'd run to a different corner of the yard, which, for no discernible reason, was preferable.

The curious thing was that they never figured out how to use the animals, how to make a spectacle of them. And yet they couldn't stop looking.

THE FOREST FLOOR

This is a landscape that has difficulty breathing. The city blocks, extending to the ocean in one direction and the desert in the other, look as if they have been soaked in brine and then desiccated, as if, should you lick a wall or signpost, your tongue would shrivel with salt. It is impossible to exaggerate the extremity of the colors. "Bleach" and "Electrical Storm" come close. There are occasional breaks in the concrete, and in these breaks one might find buildings, a bus stop, a telephone pole coated in creosote, or a tree—a good spot to chain a bike or a dog. In the homes on these blocks, trees create perspective in oil paintings, the backgrounds for Olan Mills family portraits, and the frames of children's drawings, tree to the far left, tree to the far right.

In the middle of this landscape—building after squat building, grid of wire and streetlight, billboard and burrito shack—sat a gallery. The people who ran it thought art happened in every way except five feet from something hanging on a wall. They wanted to offer visitors gifts—

cheerful, indispensable surprises. The gallery subsisted on a host of government grants, a few major donors with peculiar ideas, and a pneumatic tube at the entrance that sucked up proffered bills of any denomination along with the occasional napkin sketch, i.o.u., or burger wrapper.

Not long ago they decided to turn the gallery into a forest for a month.

Creating an uncannily convincing forest involved live plants, saplings, soil, and thick trunks with leafy branches to stand in for full-grown trees. Though admittedly log is to tree as pork is to pig, it was a necessary concession: uncut, living trees would have required removal of the roof. These giants were the first to be loaded in—great logs screwed to stands that would be concealed by the forest floor. The branches and bark shed during loading looked like litter on the sidewalk.

The amount of soil brought in was staggering—literally, it made them stagger—and it was densely inhabited: bugs, pods, worms, rot, a serious and complex smell. Everyone shifted a little under the scent. If their ears could cock, they would be cocked.

They brought in the undergrowth: dead leaves, twigs, rocks, a hollowed-out stump, ferns and grasses. In the gallery blender, previously used for cocktails and fruit drinks, they pureed bits of moss with yogurt and spread it on the downiest part of the forest to coax the moss to spread. People loitered outside, trying to resist their curiosity with the habitual diffidence of their posture.

Even before the opening, there were changes. For example, they could no longer drink soda in the office lest a nose-to-tail line of ants form from the forest to the lip of the can. They found a few beetles in the filing cabinet.

While they had expected a light infestation, they had not expected the birds. In the first week, they found a starling in the forest. Fitting, but not entirely surprising—every building gets one every now and then. But by the second week, representatives of more species had joined them—woodpecker, blue jay, finch. By the third week, a nesting pair of wrens.

Surely visitors were engaging in a bit of guerilla artistry, smuggling birds in and letting them go. Well, birds needed bugs and seeds, no? The gallery people brought in live grasshoppers from the reptile emporium and planted some late-stage sunflowers.

It was a hit—a record number of visitors for the month. People came in blinking from the street at all times of day: singly, to lounge under the trees, slip into a childhood nap; or in small groups with picnic baskets, binoculars for the birds. One day, a school bus pulled up outside, and an hour later they were plucking children from the leafy tops of trees and picking Now and Later wrappers out of the loam. They held events: talks on art and ecology and elves, a midnight screening of *The Howling*, scavenger hunts. A storyteller recited folktales about the sweetness and trouble between humans and forests. Forest as shelter, forest as test, eyes in the branches, branches hiding trail markers, the erasure of home. Visitors lingered, had trouble finding their way to the door. More money than ever was sucked through the pneumatic tube, as well as scraps of paper with smiley faces, impromptu poems no one wanted to read. They extended the show another month.

————

And on the morning of the third month, when they began the de-install, they encountered a few curious things:

1. A raccoon had built a nest in one of the stumps, and a cursory inspection solved the mystery of missing supplies from the office. Pen, paperclip chain, letter opener, reading glasses.
2. What appeared to be new branches on several trees fanned toward a skylight.
3. The tree trunk closest to the front door, where they intended to start the breakdown, and which had been quite heavy but not impossible to transport on the way *in*, now would not budge.

Each trunk the same: there was no way to push it over, no way to even rattle it. Digging in the dirt at the base, they found worms and spores, but they could no longer find the stands to which the trunks had been attached. They couldn't, in fact, find the floor. They retreated, considered. Was this a battle? And, if so, did they really want to win? They tried to wonder *how*, but their minds veered repeatedly and settled on *what*. There were the birds, the raccoon, people who came on their lunch hour with a book.

They couldn't have imagined their sanguinity two months before. It had been a gallery for ten years; it had been their life's work. They looked at one another and shrugged. So, now it would be a forest, with a door.

DEVELOPMENT

The developers left a fringe of trees around the perimeter. The Nature Trail, it was called, and houses that backed up onto it were meant to cost many dollars more than the homes in the interior. They poured concrete basements, nailed in plywood roofs and floors and laced the hollow walls with pipes, wires, and air ducts, all with the lowest warranties. They clothed them with drywall, faux brick, and vinyl siding, screwed in boilers and air filtration systems. They moved quickly and in waves, knowing they would never live there. There was a gate at the entrance, automatic arms stuck, for now, in the vertical position.

They made brochures featuring the client's three choices for every feature and finish: three bathroom and kitchen tiles, three countertops, three living-room light fixtures, and so on. Technically, they could build forty communities with not one house exactly the same as another. This was their favorite sales trivia.

They stacked these brochures and the many swatch books in the office of what they called the model home, which looked to be inhabited by golf enthusiasts. They be-gan to receive visitors into their home, careful never to sell but to evaluate—*We would love to see you in one of our homes, but we'll have to see. They've been so popular—moving in is arriving.* Then the developers were gone. Phone lines were dis-connected, urgent letters stamped "Return to Sender." The heads of automatic sprinklers poked up over grassless lawns.

Six months later, the artists came. The twenty-foot atriums, tiered ceilings, interior balconies, and Jacuzzi-sized tubs—who could put these to better use? The plan was to move into the empty houses for a month and make things. The opening was held the night after they arrived. A few murals were already sketched out. With spray paint, someone had filled the interior of a gray Cape with a coral reef and was working moonscapes onto the vinyl exterior. Another had sequestered himself in the basement of the smallest house and was playing the pipes and boiler. The visitors had to listen hard for the sounds haunting the house. The smart wiring in a columned Colonial had been tricked out to strobe the lights.

In the atriums, the artists placed buckets of ice with flip-top beers. The audience brought ornate flasks, danced a bit when there was music. But the artists never stopped work-ing, because viewing finished pieces was not the object; the artists themselves were the art.

The plan was for a month-long exhibit after the opening. Continual generation. They would stay open ten hours a day, seven days a week; cameras in every room would offer a twenty-four-hour live feed.

———

People tuned in to see: how would they survive in the half-done suburbs? They slept on plywood floors with thin blankets brought from home. They heated coffee grounds and cans of beans over Bunsen burners on granite countertops. They washed their clothes with bar soap in the bathtubs and strung them throughout the houses. Or they did not wash them. And they got to work.

To be sure, murals eventually spread over the walls. But they also placed sticks in Morse code across property lines. They rigged a pulley system between the second stories and passed drawings house to house—when you received a drawing, you had to replicate it and pass the copy to the next house. They hung drywall sculptures from the eaves and porch pillars. They made a quilt of swatches and tied it to the front gate. The floors of one house became a branching hopscotch game—into the bathroom, kitchen, up the loft stairs. One could not move inside without throwing a marker. They played House Leapfrog: drop down through the basement window of the first house, crawl up through the opposite window, scale the roof of the next house, run across and down the other side. Basement, roof, basement, roof, all the way around, one game of hopscotch in the middle.

A newspaper article covered the opening. Visitors came, mostly from the city, mostly on weekends. They would bring offerings in lieu of admission—a glue gun, decorative paper, toilet paper, fishing line, bells, a quart of fresh strawberries, a box of Ho-Hos, chalk, fresh bread, fresh solder, bottles of water and gin, canned peaches which went unopened.

A month went by, six months. They forgot to leave. Their art deepened, but their audience thinned. Sometimes in the evening, after closing, they would gather in the model house where there were no cameras and take turns straightening their backs along the forest-green couches and the fresh chemical carpet. They would talk about their lives before, which were becoming a little fuzzy. But the model home was not a place to stay for long, not a nest with the scents of themselves and their quarry.

At night they foraged for firewood in the fringe of trees and took turns reciting myths of origin around the flames.

YEAR 3

We were living in a set of stories—some we stumbled into, some too familiar, and some we did not understand—when it seemed as if we heard a narrator saying, "And it came to pass that the woman grew with child." We balked. We thought no, we will not have a baby because we are so happy and so doomed. We thought yes, we will have a baby because we want to take it camping, though we live in a metropolis and own no tent. No, yes, no, yes.

We thought of the unknown half-life of Styrofoam and Zoloft and Atrazine, and thought no. We thought of Petri dishes growing skin cultures, and thought yes. We walked in the early morning snow after a blizzard, the city so hushed we forgave ourselves for thinking we were the survivors of disaster. Then a lone skier shush-shushed her way up the middle of the street, and we thought yes. We walked into a bodega, saw the headline CITY CLEAN-UP: 1 MILLION PER INCH, and thought no.

We asked others. A friend said people were selfish until they had a baby, and we thought no. One of our mothers could think of no reason to have a baby, and we thought yes. A friend said life was better with noise and chaos, and we thought maybe not. Another said, just think *of being able to love and shape another person, and we thought no, no, no. We saw a documentary about diving babies—there they were in an ordinary chlorinated pool, swimming underwater like otters, their parents' torsos static and doughy beside them—and we thought yes.*

ANIMAL POLLINATOR

Cultivation aside, every pollinator is an accidental pollinator, the marriage of plants' limitations—rooted there, right there—and a good idea that stuck, that sticks. Insect antennae and fuzz. Bird wing and beak. Mammal and marsupial fur. Wind's dumb and constant urgency. Human sleeve.

The man visits trees and flowers all over the Alps. Careful with collection bags, scraping and tapping. He lopes back to his cabin in the evening, leans over a sheet of waxed paper, cleans himself out; if he were a cat, a wasp, it would be arm over head, arm over head. The grains fall (some always escape), each variety impossibly complex—like snowflakes, but richly meaty, tiny spangled balls. He then sorts them with pincers and a magnifying glass into outsized mason jars. The grains are nearly invisible until they are many, and then they're golden, orange, lemon chartreuse. He blows pure gold into his handkerchief at night.

————

He lives with the jars for years. Sometimes they make him feel how quickly his life is passing. Time flowing out of him, easy as morning urine. It's an indulgence, though, to think one's feelings are the only thing that bring meaning to biology.

For a long time, the levels hardly seem to rise. Late summer, fall, winter, he gathers other things. Like a trapper checking his lines, a hawk following the riverbank fields: a creature too. He dissolves into the hills each day, collects tufts of fur from fences, bark, rocks, kill sites, separates them into sheep, fox, rabbit, goat, deer, groundhog, bear. Once, black strands with a primordial, phantom stench. The tweezers shook under the magnifying glass and the tuft got its own jar, marked with a "?" There is likely an answer to the question, but that is all the answer it will get.

He collects seeds, but it's almost too easy, a vacation. The seeds make themselves obvious so as to be eaten, picked up, blown. Like taking vegetables from someone else's well-tended garden. They are fat fruits, the ones that have made it this far.

In winter, he gathers ice crystals, which turn to tiny puddles the moment he enters his banked-fire cabin. Every time. Jars with droplets of water that hold an echo of chiseled radiance but can never reassemble it. No one ever sees this bit of art.

One year, the jars of pollen look suddenly full. It is time to answer the museum's letters.

———

He brings the jars to the museum nocturnally, as the daylit noise of the city is too much. The back door, the service stairs. No one is there. Emergency exit signs light the spiral rotunda. He finds the empty platform in a nook in the wall, exactly where they wrote it would be. There is his name—his name?—on a plaque. He imagines what it would be to find it in Braille as well. What is significant fits under a fingerpad. He runs his finger over nothing—his name?—and then sets to work, many jars with tightly fitting lids slipped past customs. He had a letter from the museum, but that was not a conversation he could have, a set of actions he could stand next to: people in uniforms swirling latex fingers in the jars, pouring them onto a stainless-steel table. A dog, perhaps, with a terribly specific nose. He had a passport with his name, letters with many names, and jars of something that he did not yet understand after these many years.

Each color grain is poured onto a separate spot on the platform and shaped into a delicate cone. The golden-golden grains become the largest, the reddish-golden the middle size, the yellow-gold the smallest. If he breathes a human breath while he works, some grains will scatter in a mist, some will sift into his lungs; he will lose a year's work. He has trained his breathing to go subcutaneous, just as he's trained the steadiness of his hands. An insect, an animal concentration, like an ant building a many-chambered palace for the queen, or a bird preparing for hours the ground that will host his courtship dance.

———

He isn't courting. And he isn't sure why this is the end of the story, except that an end was needed. Other animals would come to look at these years of blooming, ignited in their nook.

This question is often a millimeter away if one is looking at something other than a canvas or a figure: How is this art? (It is never the question of the person who made it. But a person who makes a thing, or gathers a thing, or sees how others might see a thing as if for the first time, gives up that thing entirely when he puts it on display.)

Certainly, in the following weeks, some people walked by as if the nook were an empty store window. Some paused, but not long enough for a single grain to stick. Many stopped before the cones for a long time and perhaps that question did not coalesce.

For those who paused, a swarm of other thoughts. People imagined inching an index finger inside, not to deface but to touch the center, or perhaps to test the perfection of the cone, or to examine the color of the one, withdrawn finger.

They thought about labor—every grain!—with horror, perhaps, or admiration. And the vague sense that somehow, in this case, in the labor lay the art. The cones: the collection they required was both super- and subhuman: who could do such a thing without losing, by degree, the human race?

People stood with stopped breath for longer than they would have guessed. Some might worry (for how long? years? as many years as it took to collect the grains?), that they had not looked long enough. Or, surely, that they had never really seen it.

THE FRAME AROUND IT

Galleries separate objects from the world, hold them briefly, say *precious thing, you are not like other things,* then send them off to homes or collections or offices or storage and pretend no knowledge of dust adhering to resin, paper curling from collage, maps as fads this year—design and not art.

But first, galleries give objects gifts—the right angle of wall meeting wall, a soaring ceiling, the privilege of their sole attention. While clean works sometimes look too clean, dirty and wild works might seem wiser, less fleeting, the contrast layering the tone.

On Saturday, we walked into a gallery that was also a ru-ined barn except the barn had fallen to bits and the bits had been taken up by a tornado and blasted into the walls or frozen in a swirl on the floor. Still, the shadow of a barn or workshop stood around us, an organized past that had come unbound. Charred bits, broken bits, fragments of fragmented plywood, sticks, harness, rope, crate, and then file, nail, saw, all devoured by rust. Nostalgia like a giant magnet lifting the pieces and holding them in place. Rotted saddle, roots coming out of the wall.

One of our fathers lives in a twenty-foot-square cabin made of rough-hewn boards at the edge of the woods. On one wall, above the mini fridge, hot plate, and microwave in which he cools, warms, and vibrates his food, he has hung perhaps fifty antiquated kitchen utensils, the kind that were used more than a hundred years earlier in farmhouses and cabins at the edges of woods. Little wall is visible behind the display; the tools threaten in their proliferation. Cherry pitters, egg beaters, cornbread molds, various sharp or smooth, tin or wooden tools about which he will say, suddenly, Can you guess what they used this for?

We cannot guess.

Perhaps it goes without saying that he lives alone in the cabin at the edge of the woods. That he has saved his father's welding equipment, his father born in 1905 and twenty-one years dead. That he built his fireplace out of bricks salvaged from a mill fire. That he has a collection of figures his daughter fashioned out of modeling clay at eight, fingerprints embedded: dog as doctor, dog as fisherman, dog as street vendor pushing a cart overloaded with tiny colored spheres. They are covered in the dirt and dust that penetrates boxes.

There is a house up the road where his grandfather was raised, swallowed now by trees, those trees swallowed by trees. The floor cannot be trusted. Clothes ringer, wood-burning stove are visible from the windows. Who knows what is on the second floor—the stairs would eat our thighs. Glass from the window frames is sand once again. He does not own the house. It breaks his heart, the rot of the childhood home, not his childhood. He lives in his gallery and there is no sun-marked door to the street.

There were a number of pieces, variations on a theme—another gift of a gallery. In one room, an entire wall of frames as if it were a portrait collection. Frame around a charred stick, frame around a cracked leather strap, the hoop from an undone bucket, a worn-handled awl. These things are famous, too.

In the next room, there was a mound made of tree roots, shards of pressed wood, frayed rope, and other binders not binding. The whole swelling together as if assembling. Like a brain rising from a bowl of neurons. A Frankenstein past, memory in the cells. A thing wants to be but the universe does not want it to. Humans want a thing but they cannot keep it whole. Sometimes, knowing this, they want it, safely, after it is nearly gone.

The artist has taken the ruin from the past and the ruin yet to come and slid them into the smooth present, the one that knows how to plaster a wall, keep the flood waters low, quell the fire (almost) before it starts. This is, of course, the story the present tells itself. But here comes the charred stick. The white paint, the wall of sun-stunned windows, the covert climate control—they let the stick in, they light it well.

In real life, the tools' loneliness, their display, can cripple you. They can't mend or carry or hold or make any longer.

But this is the best gift the gallery can give: for a month, nostalgia swells with knowingness. The sticks gesture, they stir up a dust cloud that stings the eye, and yet when it enters the mouth, it is delicious. We cannot say, but if we had to say...no, we couldn't. The objects are too much themselves, irreducible, until they are not.

SOLITUDE

She was showing photographs of herself standing, crouching, lying in ruins. Art has always loved a ruin—on a far hill the gauzy chateau in a swoon of bricks, the barn listing out from under its paint. The ruins art now loves are industrial, the places we have made that threaten to undo us.

She worked through the slides. A defunct subway line with standing water hosting the ghosts of typhus and cholera. She has forded the water and is touching a slick brick wall, her face turned from the camera. A receding darkness suggests eyeless fish.

The next photograph shows an ownerless factory with swollen machines that might have come from an inquisitor's chamber. The bodies that grew to fit the machines are no longer needed. She stands at a broken window past a bay of rust and serrated edges. Her body is unmarked.

A drowned and ragged shipyard. We could see without seeing the submerged hulls, winches, boards, pilings, the years of cargo slopped overboard. We could see, too, as she stood in the shallows, how persistent and looming the wreckage—this was no longer a place for human bodies. She was supposed to have walked on and not looked back.

She is lying on a metal tray in the hall of an abandoned hospital that looks as though it has long been given over to apes. Her body seems bound for the morgue—it says, *that moment when we thought there was a cure, that moment is ready for an autopsy.*

A rail yard has leaked rust into the air. She is balanced on a train track, but as if she knows it is sinking and will take with it the stone and the boxcars and the history of the twentieth century.

In all of these photos, she was naked. And at first we thought, oh, she's naked, and then we thought, oh she's naked. Which meant that immediately we did what we weren't supposed to (or were we?) and looked at her in front of us. We tried to slip off her clothes. But something about her distance from us in the photos or the way she angled her body did not let us think we'd actually seen her nakedness.

Then we started to get a little scared. Because she had been alone and naked where we imagine bodies get dumped. These places no longer follow any rules—they might hold dangers criminal, physical, or supernatural. They can't wait to wound us. And she lay down in these places and got them all over her. We were afraid for her, afraid for her naked feet that must have been burned or cut or eaten away.

And then, suddenly, we were a little afraid *of* her. As if these ruins had taken up residence in a future without us. They are the places our grandchildren will pick through for food or tools. She is already the next generation of human, with abilities beyond ours and no need for clothes. She does not smile for the camera; she doesn't even look our way.

But we liked being scared like this. When we're scared by something and don't like it, we tend not to call it art. But this—we were grateful to her for finding the empty, vengeful places and making them beautiful for us. These were some of the loneliest places we'd seen, and she walked into them like the last person on earth. Only with a camera, so she wasn't entirely alone. We were with her, we got it! The human body devoured by its own wreck; the body emerging, surviving the machinations created by the human brain. She gave us the past and the future in one flash.

Her photos got us to agree to many things: that we have made places that make our bodies cringe and we will someday pay for this. That we would not scour her nakedness in a pornographic way. That, though she was alone in the photos, alone in the bowels of the city, she was now in a room full of people who loved her. And people bought her images. We'd heard it earned her a living. She probably didn't have to wait tables or stand on the sidewalk with a clipboard or otherwise hustle and scrounge. And, unlike the factory or the port or the rail yard, art was a functioning economy, at least for a few. Half the earth was a looming wreckage, but it was not yet time to be afraid.

And then a young man raised his hand. "In that picture," he said, and pointed to a shot of a sugar factory filled with snow through its missing roof. She is perched, naked of course, on the steps wound around a towering vat, her feet buried in the snow. "In that picture, how did you get that much sugar everywhere?"

The room paused. And then laughed. Because surely this was an odd joke. No one could imagine that the old factory still held that much sugar, and that she had staged a kind of gingerbread fantasia. He misunderstood the irony of sugar turned to snow. Was he not with us? Did he think she had fabricated these places? Had he misunderstood everything? How much we enjoyed the real terror of our failures; how little we thought we had to do with creating them; how we agreed that we would only have to make pictures of their consequences. But he was serious. Where we saw danger, he saw sweetness. And when we laughed, he stood and then fled.

After that night, people remembered her body, her minnow-belly body flashing between annihilation and imperviousness. It was the perfect expression of a future we fear, where we cannot clothe ourselves against the past.

But we remembered, too, the young man's mistake, how he ran from the room. To see the wrong thing so clearly is what we fear of the present. And to be alone in the machinery of the night on the wrong side of an unbroken window.

ARTIFACT

We saw a photograph in the newspaper of a streetlight—intact, still straight, but half-buried in the ground. We saw its shape, its function, its implied ubiquity and height; we were aware, suddenly, of streetlights buzzing lightly in curves and grids around the globe, all because it was half-buried. That is, in the photograph, the infrastructure of the present had been turned into an artifact. The caption said it was part of an art installation that would not last forever, so we got up, filled a water bottle from the tap, packed some energy bars, and walked into the world to court an uncertain relationship to our eyes.

The subway, which runs right past our window before it disappears into the side of a hill, took us to the end of our island, where people gather to glimpse a statue we have forgotten how to see as improbable, rising out of complex and turbulent headwaters. We stood in a chute with other day-trippers until a woman in uniform opened the gate, then we rushed to a ferry that would take us to a smaller island. Though we'd passed dozens of streetlights on the way, the one we were after was somewhere ahead.

The ferry's engine owned us through the soles of our feet, and we moved as one vibration across the channel. We had read of the repercussions of sound waves on sea creatures, but we did not remember to consider this at the time—the engine throbs moving through mussel beds, pipefish, cormorants in a dive. Behind us, the metropolis began to look more and more like a photograph of itself. Could people really be casually intimate with the interior of every window on every floor? Could we really have shuttled underneath the length of the island? Unseen, outdated pumps work every moment to keep the sea from reclaiming the tunnels, its salt marshes. We did not think of this then, we do not or try never to think of it.

As the island seemed to rise up out of the water and surge toward us, we realized we knew nothing about where we were going. All we had was a name, Governors Island, and our bag of food and drink, which would not last more than a few hours. In another era, the lack of preparation might have qualified as a fatal error in judgment; in this, we felt it was a lark.

Governors Island revealed itself to us in strata like a horizontal archeological dig. Where we disembarked, a facsimile of a party beach had been installed, with a sound stage, stands with endless ketchup, volleyball nets, and sand trucked in from wherever there may have been a perceived surfeit of sand. Young professionals in sandals had gathered in a crowd. A contemporary entertainment, the out-of-place ecosystem: Virginia Beach in New York City, NYC in Las Vegas, an ice hotel in Dubai, the gardens of Babylon in the Arizona desert.

Moving into the interior, a sign told us that the squat stone building ahead was once a colonial customs building— remarkable in a country with a passion for razing and rebuilding, for fabricating natural phenomena. We could have learned more, but we were looking to match the image from the newspaper, now stored in our minds, to one in the landscape.

We pressed on and walked awhile beside a high chain-link fence topped with a swirl of razor wire. Behind the chain-link were spare, sixties-era apartment blocks that a sign identified as former Air Force family housing. We registered the warning the fence implied, our pulse alert: something was either being protected or quarantined. Through the wire we saw playgrounds where plastic sandbox toys had outlasted the rusted slides. We saw, too, a cut in a fence, a tuft of fabric, broken ground-floor windows, symbols spray-painted on the walls. We wondered who might be looking through the fence from the other side and how long they'd been there.

Farther, beyond a grassy park (in which we gratefully rested, ate dense packets of nutrition, struggled in and out of hammocks, and stared up at the sky, feeling we could be anywhere at any time), we took a path bisecting the island and finally saw signs for the art installation. We entered a low, sleek building and quickly realized we'd also entered the artists' conceit. Vitrines filled with artifacts and placards explained that the remains of an isolated settlement on the island had recently been discovered. In the 1700s, a group of immigrants had settled the island, and, like moths in a niche climate, it had evolved unique features. The settlers developed their own dialect and customs—they revered birds, for example, and were ceramicists by trade—before finally dying out in the 1950s, their remains undiscovered until now.

On our way to the adjacent dig, we were handed white hard hats and orange safety vests, asked to humor the conceit in this and other ways. In the field there was a bell tower operated by a foot treadle; we climbed in and gamely pumped until a beautiful peal spilled down. A diner hunkered in the dirt; inside, an excavated jukebox that still spun fifties crooners. The taillights of a junked car flickered under heavy fins. We saw everywhere confirmation of the narratives spun by the museum display—the defunct bird houses, shards of pottery, framed portraits in the diner of its final, tragic owners.

We were amused, had a good time, took pictures of ourselves in hard hats, junior archaeologists, all. But we had wanted to be knocked from behind our eye sockets. Instead, we were fenced inside someone's clever idea. We wandered on, inert, until at the edge of the field we found the image from the newspaper: a streetlight half-submerged in the dirt and the top half of a telephone pole beside it, as if a wave of mud had rolled down an ordinary street and hardened. Half-bury something—something normally in full-view—and we will see even more than we had forgotten how to see. We will see into the future, see ourselves as past.

We took off our protective gear and left the installation behind; we walked, nursing our disappointment, mentally paring down the exhibit to just those few plain objects.

Streetlight, telephone pole, and…? We tried to fill in a list of things we can no longer see. But we can no longer see them. We wanted half-buried objects that might show us who we are: creatures in the middle of a bramble who think we are in a meadow. Clear views of brambles ahead and behind, optical fatigue in the yawning now.

Suddenly, yes suddenly, we were walking not through fields but along a weedy avenue of homey Armed Forces duplexes that had likewise been abandoned. At the end of the road was a strange sight: branches growing through second-story windows of one duplex *from the inside out*. Trees had taken up residence inside a house barely thirty years old. We thought of seeds everywhere, dormant or sprouting— on roofs, in mortar, tire treads, awnings, in the baskets of strollers with a little sand, a little spilled milk, between the knuckles of dogs, even under our beds, growing with fairy- tale speed up through the mattresses and through our ribs, light-seeking. The air on the broken avenue held sound in reserve; the ground felt full of muscle memory.

When we finally looked away—because we had to look away—we saw the open sea extending ad nauseam. We were at the far end of the island. We were out of rations. When we heard the warning bell, we ran for the last ferry home.

WE'RE COMING FOR THEM

I. We had been waiting for something in the city. As if our lives hadn't started yet. Likely it was static from the Judeo-Christian tradition—a savior always about to come (back)—or a Cold War hangover, or nerves over dirty bombs and nuclear reactors. There was also a First World anticipation—surely something good, and then even better, was coming our way. We had been taking pictures of cornerstones, selling pretty well, barely registering the irony—as if a photograph of a foundation might itself be a foundation.

We went out in the country where our lives did not exist, and a friendly local asked us if we wanted to see something that was really something? Built by the town crazy. Like nothing we'd see in the city? We did. We brought our cameras.

Way back in sand dunes of scrub cedar and sumac sat a pole barn raised by hand and built of scrap—a sheet of fiberglass here, bleached pine there, washed-up life preservers tacked everywhere.

Inside the barn, there is no other way to say it, was a flying saucer. Plywood had been warped into the classic shape—a disc body with a cockpit bubble on top, round porthole windows dotting the upper side. The exterior was painted blue, blue like the bottom of a swimming pool, like a clear sky. Perhaps it was camouflage: we would never see it when it rose.

A hatch door swung down. "Go on, climb up. He won't mind," our guide said.

Carpet remnants made the interior feel like a basement rec room. A swivel barstool rose up into the cockpit and was surrounded by a nest of electronics. We were supposed to believe in the blinking lights, the whir that slowly rose to match the whir in our heads. There were coolers wedged into the perimeter, some topped with cushions to make seats, a small library in another area—medical textbooks, how-to for horticulture and electronics, programming, ham radio. A locked box contained, our guide said, offerings for when it landed.

The builder had covered the inside of the barn with mirrors, and when full-length mirrors emptied his savings, our guide also told us, the man filled in with salvaged mirrors from junked trailers, estate sales, even rearview mirrors from scrapyard cars pieced together across the walls and ceiling. In the world of the barn, the spaceship was everything.

This kind of waiting was finished with the earth and all that we might make of it. We set to work.

Word got out that we were looking for them, the secret builders. We heard of another and then another, in places people called "the middle of nowhere"—a misnomer as "nowhere" proliferated. We rented cars and drove through state after state, trickled down capillary country roads. We couldn't shoot fast enough. It seemed almost too easy: a rocket, an orb, a disc, a disc, a disc. Fiberglass, resin, aluminum, plastic, canisters of helium and propane and oxygen. Automotive toolkits, wires, lights, and faith that when the time is right, the body will rise.

Mostly, the spaceship builders did not come out of their trailers or houses, though our local guides claimed they didn't mind the occasional tour. They were so serious they could not see that others might laugh. Some of their grounds looked measured and neat, some were spilling over or scraped to dust. Most builders were single, a few married, some widowed or divorced. The married ones interested us most—what sorts of agreements had they come to? Were the ships built for two?—but we never met a wife. Most made regular visits to the hardware store where they either stared at their bellies and handed over a list, or they followed the clerk down the aisles and watched over the sawing of boards and the plucking of hinges and screws. Most got checks from the State, some had been in the Service, some had tried to live in a City and hurried home—all monoliths they wanted to escape. Some wrote stories for local newspapers about places they'd never been; some came to their town's operettas in pressed shirts, hat lines in their hair; some brought finished puzzles to the drugstore to be laminated. This is what the towns could see of them. Mostly they retracted from the main roads, back through trees and tall grasses, to spots where the stars looked personal. There the builders might see and be seen by the only eyes that mattered.

We learned all of this from the local guides, whose tab we picked up at their favorite bar or with whom we cruised the town and back roads. As our guides gave up the details, they usually seemed a little proud of their native loony. Proud, perhaps, that his version of loony was so ambitious. Sometimes the local just laughed—the spaceman really did belong on another planet—and gave a knowing look: he's not like us, you and me. But sometimes the local might eventually say, sure, the guy was crazy, but if you listened closely, if you looked at his notebooks and his drawings, who knows, maybe he was the smartest guy around. Da Vinci came up a few times, his flying machines—what was the difference between the two? What were we missing? The local looked up, eyes surprised, a little feverish, before he knocked the thought back with a drink.

We couldn't say how sad warped plywood and wires hooked up to nothing made us. We couldn't explain it, so we took pictures instead.

We shot every angle and vantage point—entry holes, fuel tanks, gaps in the construction, rain-swollen walls. We climbed trees and roofs to look down on the machines, got low among the biting things to frame a rocket nose against the sunrise.

Among the many shots, a slight motif emerged: spaceships in reflection. The first was the mirrored barn, of course. The next was in a salt marsh, standing water everywhere, pitcher plants in siren clusters. The ship was an orb hung on wires between tall poles, and, when it was weighted just so, it could zip from one end of the property to the other. The puddles, the water in the throats of the plants, reflected the sky and the brief flicker of a spaceship tethered to Earth. The spaceship in a puddle was at once bobbing in the sky and boring into the ground.

Then another ship reflected in a truck's rearview mirror, another in the sunglasses of our guide. Through the lens, the ships looked more mysterious, the fantasy more possible, but also more remote, inaccessible to the eye. That was the hope anyway.

II. Eventually we came home, hauled ourselves up many stairs to our berth. We lived for a short time then in the undeveloped film, in each field and barn and scrapyard. We ordered in, we carried sacks of laundry down and then up the stairs, taxis and subway cars dropped us at predetermined locations. People of all description met our needs, or approximately so; in other words, we were back in the city. All the while, we hung back in the film, testing out the minds of the builders. Their presumed hope was: to be on the Earth but not of it—a religious impulse—and then, more and more, neither of the Earth nor on it.

But within weeks, the city had seeped back in and we were irretrievably post-marsh, post–night sky, post–distant neighbor, post–lone visionary. We could not all have pole barns, could not all go up. But there are many ways to hover, and this time the irony did register: in the city we rarely considered that there was ground under our feet, and the information that we stood on the unstable crust of one planet among millions did not seem to apply to us. We, and eight million others, moved about as if in a futurist drawing.

At the opening, red dots accumulated in the catalogue with breathtaking swiftness. People looked as if they were seeing something on the wall and in their minds, and then in the air when they looked away. The volume rose in the room minute by minute. We felt very famous and ashamed for that one night. The excitement of others sparked a greediness in us, the slippery thought that what we had been waiting for was our own brilliance. All night we tracked that brilliance reflected in the glass and the eyes around us.

For a few days, there was a flurry of activity—sales, commissions, offers to tour the show. One reporter wanted to write a profile of us. She revealed over coffee what she had dug up: our high school transcripts, photographs we took that ran in our college papers or hung still in a department-store portrait studio, a few former landlords and lovers—the odd trail we didn't know we'd left behind.

And then there were the reviews. One critic said our images captured the curdled American Dream. This was the painful, salted beauty of second, third, fourth-generation immigrants readying for another great exodus to a promised land. We had captured every angle of desire and the dead-end stories it tells.

Another critic, a bigger magazine, said we offered a shallow lampoon of Heartland America. That we made light of the thwarted ambitions of people stuck in a disposable economy. That perhaps these builders were the artists and we the coarse bullies who tore them down.

We carried these words with us everywhere we went, darts under the skin. You don't know us, we said on walks, in line at the bakery. You don't know how rich our empathy, how full our tone. We do not come by love easily, but we have learned to respect effort and the airless panic of failure. We took so many pictures of it. How could you fail to see?

III. Cause and effect are notoriously difficult to establish. We'll just mention proximity instead: about a month after the show, we engaged a realtor, a guide to the outermost of the outer boroughs. She kept her face impassive and found what we required—just a shell, really, with loose zoning regulations.

The neighborhood buzzed, but with subterranean machines, not with people. There were many more bolt locks than windows per block, and when a dog barked, we understood from the echo that it was not standing on grass. Nothing rose above the utility poles, as if they murmured, "Bow down," and the buildings complied. In other words, the perfect place to begin.

We left our cameras napping in their plush cases; we left behind our memory foam mattresses, too, though we spent both days and nights in the new warehouse among piles of lumber and fiberglass and scrapyard treasures. We became builders. Yes, we could see the way this would play, the way our ship would become a destination, how visitors would tick off the references: Noah, da Vinci, Columbus, Orville and Wilbur, and Bucky Fuller—all outsiders let in (by virtue of being right)—plus a little Dr. Frankenstein, a little Heaven's Gate. Late sixties/early seventies starmen songs would be playing softly in the background, and plastering the inside of the garage would be images of biospheres, cryogenics, floating cities, unexplained flying objects, jetpacks, motherhsips. It would be called an installation in the broadside and advertisements: open to the public, with a shuttle from the midtown museum. People would love to crawl up inside, push pretend buttons, wait for the roof to retract, which it would at unpredictable intervals, and count down to zero.

We have built a roof that retracts (and, of course, leaks when it rains), but we can see at most two stars on the clearest of nights. We will not show this when we're done. We are, instead, tending to a private urge: to gather all of our ambition, misanthropy, and fear—they are inseparable, really—in a disc and turn them ridiculous and cozy. When we finish, we will climb up in the evenings to drink our tea or a beer, take in the city haze reflected back to us, and imagine what we might look like from a great distance.

YEAR 4

We read a book about the many "wedges" scientists and law-makers would have to introduce in order to slow global warming and avert environmental catastrophe. Each year we noticed that none of the last-chance-must-exit wedges had been driven in. The thick part of an infinitely increasing y axis was bearing down on us, but we were suddenly three in a strange configuration—one body and another body with a body inside of it. It was easy in this year to become a composite ball, and to tap on the ball in the middle and say the name of the future.

Then the we that was a body with a body inside of it drove to a museum in another state, and on the way the skies turned weird and opened up. We pulled to the side of the road, climbed into the backseat, and fell into a deep sleep while the car shook with rain. Which seemed an apt metaphor for the year.

At the museum, we saw trees in large metal drums suspended in the air between utility poles. The drums were upside down, though, and the trunks strained sideways, trying to right themselves. Which seemed an apt metaphor for the repercussions of human whim.

BOUNTY

The wolf's lips are raised in a snarl, its head lowered as if assessing its prey. There is enough wild in us to feel patches of hair rise on the backs of our necks, and enough tame to enjoy the feeling. Only the wolf is inside, under the lights, and we are outside in the dark. Only it's stuffed and we're not standing outside a Montana bar but on the sidewalk of the latest gallery district. We have trouble telling where the danger is.

Inside, the lighting is impressive, instructive. It shows us the wolf's mouth and in the mouth a sharp incisor and on that tooth a bug that is not a bug but a winged creature crouching on its hind legs, humanoid and primal and alien at once, made of bug parts and plant parts and a whisper of twine. Its tiny wings are borrowed silver, its torso darkly segmented. It has been caught up in the age-old story of mandible over flesh—the fairy insect will be torn and washed down. We lean in, get a thrill at the delicate sacks of our eyes close to such a point, and see that the carapace creature is at war, at its shoulder the smallest arrow. This is hubris or an object lesson in ambition. Prick the gums, scale the tooth, bleed the tongue.

We look again and the story changes. In the fur of the wolf chin, reinforcements, each ascending a single hair. They are not afraid; they have been made and now they are loose and rising. They will flood the mouth, its roof ribbed like the hold of a ship. They will spike the jellied brain, nap in the nasal cavities, sip from the back of the eye until it folds.

There is a genre of American photograph featuring men in woolen pants standing for scale and satisfaction next to small mountains of fur. Inside of each fur are the bones and disarray that had been a wolf. Bounty. Special prices for wolf cubs.

They were doubtless not eligible for taxidermy, which requires animals to be killed in such a way as to make it easier to pretend they are still alive. To mount an animal, the taxidermy artist removes the skin, taking special care around the fragile areas like the eyes and nose and mouth. They take a mold of the carcass and try to capture the animal's essence, channeling its posture from the inside out. They hide the sutures, slip expensive glass spheres into their sockets. Natural history museums across Europe are full of stuffed creatures—the last pose of the last of their kind.

We have seen a live wolf twice. Once on a concrete slab in an Athens zoo, the wolf's body shrunk around its bones under the punishing heat, its face alive with flies. Once on a remote road, a dark slink crossed in front of our car and was gone.

———

Hanging from the ceiling of the gallery is a dragonfly that has been commandeered by two dark fairies. Two more give a bumblebee's fur a sharp nuzzle. It's as if they have risen from the decay they're creating: scraps of chitin, leg, and wing you'd need a magnifying glass to find. We think about what could come together from the corners of our apartments, from the sink strainer, from a drainage ditch, the foyer of a biotech company, the mud flap of a semi, cardboard box, boot heel, subway pole. Something neon with a powerful limp, and that is as far as we want to go.

In a corner, they have vivisected a bat. One pulls at its earhole. Several more look as if they are trying to learn flight from the wings fanned and pinned. They springboard from the webbing, spar in the moss below. Play is practice. In the next piece, a mouse is harvested, mummified, as if sucked dry by a score of tiny straws. From a rabbit's skull they have made a slide, a galleria, cafeteria, lounge. The creatures' very glee is menacing. Pleasure is bloody. One must seize one's object, pin it and tie it, take it from the inside, make it dance.

We leave wondering if it is possible to be every character in a fairy tale. The fanged beast already doomed, the collage of deadly parasites, multiplying their pleasures. Together we are a twenty-first century army, and we know how to tell a story.

GET YOUR KIT TOGETHER

We are visiting a parent in a low suburban grid and take a trip to a nearby sporting goods store. Since it's not our natural habitat, we begin shopping giddily: lawn games at two for the price of one; as-seen-on-TV packaging; fabric that at once warms, cools, and dries; gloves that will increase your grip on anything that comes to hand. It's summertime and we fill our cart with leisure we had not imagined, fun we must have.

And then we enter the tent aisle. We don't *need* a tent, are not going to *buy* a tent, but above the stockpiles of each model sits a miniature version of that tent fully assembled and pitched on a shelf of AstroTurf, the largest tent perhaps two feet across. Tent poles perfectly arched, functional zippers, the colors of land and men. Nothing to startle except their unexpected size. In this vast collection of goods, the tents are likely the only objects one can't buy or use, intended purely for fantasy.

We feel keenly that, through the tents, we have stepped into a new register of human experience, something unavailable in the regular-sized world. The tents imply simple interactions involving flashlights and water jugs, but also something as see-through as skin cells—an aspect of good intentions, satiety, benign repose. Nothing unworthy would survive the shrinkage required to fit in that tent. We take the tents in our hands and don't want to let them go.

That winter came on hard with what seemed like more than the usual warnings: trains frequently stopped between stations, while we spent long moments pressed up against strangers in the dark; the water from the tap turned orange and then gray without official comment; snow fell and fell one week and there was nowhere for it to go but into the river—loads of slush, trash, salt, and magnesium chloride hauled down to the banks; temperatures spiked and then plummeted, spiked and plummeted until concrete cracked; the city advised us on days we should not go outside and breathe deeply; milk and pills and baby bottles were re-called, meat and lettuce and lotion. We wanted to, but could not, stop using things, putting them in or on our bodies.

Through that long winter, our encounter with the tents stayed with us, in present tense. We would catch from time to time what seemed like the world of the tents on the periphery of our senses—a stillness in our fellow subway passenger that wasn't sleep (or death), the way a bird, a squirrel, and a park bench arranged themselves into a wel-coming tableau, the sun sliding down in the sky a little too quickly. We would feel the slight pressure of the tent in our hands, like a perched bird. Each time we felt wonder, which word embarrassed us at first until we realized it simply meant a mixture of calm and at-the-ready. We tried to spend the wonder wisely, tried to be the we who would fit into the tents, the distilled we—conscientious, non-reactive, optimistic. We tried to be kinder to the next few people we'd see, allowing for an unseen history, an uncertain future.

There was a little game we started playing at night when we were trying too hard to fall asleep: we would picture the tents *in situ* under the fluorescent lights and unreasonably high ceilings of their stores. And then we'd move them in our minds to a secluded hillside, perhaps in a state or national park, or a sculpture garden, a surprise waiting around the bend.

The collection started modestly: we found a store outside our city that had held onto outdated models of the model tents. A woman with nervous eyes led us behind the Employees Only door into an even vaster, darker area: the store behind the store. We were backstage at a circus come to town—the melancholy side of a glittery hustle.

She led us to a little area defined by a carpet remnant, lit with track lights, and filled with items that no longer had any business in the better-lit front of the store—a life-sized cutout of a family playing in the sand under a discontinued beach umbrella, a display grill with broken knobs, a stuffed bear wearing last season's rain boots. And there on the carpet, a navy family tent and a green model meant for two. They hadn't been waiting for us, but we didn't mind feeling as if they had.

The employee asked us to leave with the tents through the back exit, and, our hand on the push bar, we turned and saw the ceiling *above* the ceiling of the store, just a dark pocket of air that stretched over the store and collected the dust of a million transactions. Every mote of this space was heated in the winter, cooled in the summer. It felt like a warning, like a symbol for the dead end of effort, of optimism. But it was an actual space; it was, perhaps, a breeding ground for new and industrious cancers. No one was meant to notice this space. But we messed up; we turned and saw it. And thought of paintings of Lot's wife, the rapes of Europa and Lucretia, the sacking of Troy. Paintings that featured poses like our own: their faces turned over their shoulders in lurid, fleshy horror, witness to buildings on fire, angry gods and armies bearing down—well-lit paintings of apocalypse in marble buildings across Europe. Who would paint the cubic meters of space between the upper and lower ceilings of the sporting goods store?

That was why we were here. Because all that long winter we'd felt perpetually on the verge of turning into a pillar of salt. We tried not to look where we should not look, but increasingly it seemed there was nowhere else to look. But when we looked again at the tents, we felt a reprieve. If we picked them up and carried them out in front of us and put them in the passenger seat of our car, and never once looked away, we still had somewhere to go, wherever they belonged.

"You're not going to…hurt them, are you?" the woman asked from the edge of the light.

No, we would never.

"Do you think maybe you might put them outside, eventually?"

We hoped so, yes.

From their perches on the dining table and the couch, they released a gentle sedative. Running our hands over their nylon, easing their zippers up and down was like having a complex glass of wine at the end of the day. But the effect began to dim, and, as we had been raised in the same soil as the sporting goods store, we began to think: bigger, bigger! *We will put them to use,* we told ourselves. *Because we can't shrink to their size and we're not yet pillars of salt, we'll make a piece with them, a big installation. We'll write a proposal about artifice and escape and the spiritual kitsch we make of nature.* We collected more, from stores farther and farther away.

Each time it was the same—a man or woman in khakis and a maroon polo, admission into the dark second store. Towers of full or flattened boxes, and a little area of things that employees couldn't bring themselves to throw away, set up sometimes almost like a Christmas village. Moose in T-shirts gathered at a cardboard hearth, spokespeople cutouts towering over the model tents, arranged like the scene from a story—the pretend, for all of us, more emotionally potent than the real.

Soon we had too many tents for the living room and office and the cupboards affixed to the ceiling. We began to fill a storage unit and work out how the miniature tents would populate their meadow. For the installation, they would need a sizeable knoll surrounded by oak and pine trees, sandy soil lovers. We'd give each tent a fire pit, miniature oak and pine trees, a picnic table, and an unobtrusive campsite number. A few sites might get an extra item—a clothesline strung between trees or a tiny cooler on a picnic table, a towel with a sailboat pattern draped across a rock. These items would offer the scant evidence of habitation. The human body brushing up against its lightest enclosure.

Through the campsite we would lay roads cut from rolls of fake-pebble linoleum, wide enough for regular-sized humans to walk. The paths would take the greatest effort. They'd have to connect each campsite and offer exit and entrance from the field. We would have to think like the planner of a wealthy subdivision—how to not simply succumb to the numbing grid, how to embrace the contours of the field and make each lot a discovery? A curving main road, cul-de-sacs in graceful florets. The roads would have to offer the visitor every available irony: a subdivision made of tents; the fantasy of Nature and our proximity to it; the way the tents are both complete and waiting for occupancy. And then the visitor's own preposterous size and potential for chaos next to the tents, and their unlikely presence in the field that has been, nonetheless, made for them. The paths must make the visitors think about their shoes now walking on the vinyl pebbles, uncertain if they are allowed to step off into the grass, closer to the tent sites and their functional zippers.

We keep thinking, *We'll make a piece, we'll make a piece. The kitsch of nature* repeats satisfyingly in our heads. *Mass-market roughing it, high-tech back to nature, tent villages ancient and futuristic.* We scramble for the language of grants and statements. *We'll make a piece, we'll make a piece,* because that's how we discipline our minds, how we make ourselves give up our pleasures, our lazy fantasies, impotent outrage, the habits of mourning and fear. Because that's how we turn our minds into a showroom.

But we won't. Make. Discipline. Show. We are deep into an unnaturally warm fall, buying, eating, throwing things away, paying $89.99 a month for an urban storage unit full of tents and for the pleasure of the fantasy: we walk out on the hillside among the tents like a shepherd, then lie down at eye level. We know how to get small enough. We are in a private wilderness; we have been sniffed and accepted. We wash our faces with bracing water and spit our baking soda toothpaste behind a log. The fluid that bathes our brains is unrippled, our eyelids are smooth, our smiles calm, our four-hundred-yard gaze corralled by the tree line, the low-hanging stars. At night, before the predators emerge, we zip ourselves in.

WAKE UP, WAKE UP

We watched and watched and couldn't tell if the man in the glass casket was moving. His ribcage didn't appear to lift and fall, but neither did his skin look like putty or a milky-blue butchershop haunch. It was smooth and rosy beige, like a craft show watercolor. Dark curls draped from his head, and his limbs and torso were dotted with flowers, tough little wildflowers and orchids that browned almost perceptibly while we watched. Long grasses grew beneath his body, flattening under his torso and arcing up between his legs, making for his genitals a shaded hutch. We thought of a newborn rabbit. We thought of grown-up claws.

The shoulder nearest us was hitched slightly and his face turned away a few degrees, as if he were about to roll to his side. His second and third toes were overlong and callused, but his feet and hands did not look as if they'd seen hard use. He was thin but not gaunt, his skin unmarked, or, rather, we suspected a few pimples and a bruise were daubed with makeup. Spider-veined lids covered his still-plump eyes. His hands rested on his chest, but his elbows bent at odd angles, as if his arms had been dropped while limp. We couldn't decide if the body had arranged itself, had been arranged, or had been dumped.

The more we looked, the less we knew. The references avalanched in our minds: an Indian funeral pyre, Jesus, strippers on whose prone bodies morsels are served to businessmen, assorted fairytale heroines, prone actors discovered in city parks on police procedurals, actual bodies found in city parks. The body is in the weeds, it is a precious flower, it is naked, nude, or neutered. It is in repose or traumatized. Beyond us or beneath us.

This sudden thought arrived with conviction: everyone in the room wanted him, despite or maybe because of the fact that he might be a corpse. Like a limp and beautiful woman in the kind of advertisements that turn her face from view or crop it from the page. He would absorb the warmth of our bodies, any amount of it. We could crush the orchids; and then, after, we could pilfer his placidity, his slowed or nothing pulse under these many eyes. We don't know why we think the things we do.

At some point we had to leave because that is what you do: enter, look, and leave. A spectacle or a thought is not built to linger. On our way out, we noticed what seemed to be a bit of trash around the periphery—a half-empty water bottle, scraps of paper, candy wrappers. And we were surprised at the gallery's laxity, surprised that visitors would have disrespected the body.

———

We respected the body. Worried about it. Called it up in our minds and felt it under our palms, then felt that our palms were his palms. Over the next week, our digital clocks lit and darkened their line segments to indicate the passing of time; we repeatedly put things in our mouths and swallowed; we walked quickly here and then there; we aired more and less bearable facets of our personalities; we lived inside our laptops and our phones; once in a while we lived in a room or on the sidewalk, sometimes in a book or on a spot of grass. Then a bit of quiet would enter our perimeters and we'd half shut our eyes and find we were still in the gallery with him, our gaze tethered to his ribcage, to the brown rimming the orchids on his sternum. We imagined ourselves not pressing against him, but becoming the air or airlessness inside the glass coffin. His stillness felt vast, as if an epoch were coalescing around him, while we were mice, burning out our hearts in one season. At night, in our beds, we tried to assume the pose of the body. But our legs twitched, our minds stuttered, all the things we could not control running through us uncontrolled.

A week later, we returned to the gallery, and it seemed as if he had not moved. But neither could we detect signs of decay. We wondered about catheters and climate control, we wondered about cryogenics, if this was a body being saved for another time. Sleeping Beauty was based on the same idea—prick your finger and fall out of your moment; wake later and finish your life. If he was Sleeping Beauty, when did he go under? There was no context for the body to tell us which world he had faded from and which he would wake into. It's funny, in the story, no one asks Beauty if she remembers her life before the coma. No one asks her if she has any advice. Shouldn't someone have asked: What do you see when you see us? What do you remember that we don't?

We finally looked away and noticed the title of the show printed plainly on the wall: *Time Capsule.* We took this to mean that he's not meant for us, that he would be sent to the future. And then we noted that the items on the room's periphery had multiplied, as at the spontaneous memorials outside a dead celebrity's house. Letters, ticket stubs, a baseball cap, family photos. Amateur drawings of city monuments, the president, and what looked to be someone's dog. Flags from around the world, a digital thermometer, a stack of programs from Broadway shows, a bumper sticker with a peace sign, and another with a fish turning into an alligator turning into an ape turning into a human turning into a bird and flying away. Chess pieces, a baggie of animal fur, an MTA card, a Barbie Doll in a homemade Girl Scout uniform, a mound of unfashionable cell phones. When we saw a man add a pair of 3-D glasses with a failed sleight of hand, we went straight to the gallery's front desk, but they wouldn't tell us if the items had been left by the artists, adding a little more each day, or if visitors had left them in a kind of homage or participation or mourning. They feigned ignorance. Not that we minded, actually—we liked that we didn't know. We just didn't like that they knew and we didn't.

We went back a third time because we happened to be in the area and wanted to drop by, check in on him. No, that's not true, of course. We won't lie. We'll try not to lie. We brought something for the time capsule. Choosing items had seemed an impossible task—should we leave things of great personal meaning? But then, who could appreciate them as we did, and what if we found we couldn't live without them? Should we try for objects that define our civilization, our country, our moment? Should we try to communicate directly or try a metaphorical reaction—items that might "strike" the future viewer, or "flood," "impress," or "shock"?

This is what we brought in a reusable shopping bag: A pouch with a plastic knife/fork/spoon/napkin and corrugated containers of salt and pepper; the instruction sheet that had come wrapped around a toddler's ball: "Roll or gently toss ball to child, clap and laugh as child reaches for ball (WARNING: Do not allow child to chew on ball for any length of time)"; a travel-size bottle of hand sanitizer; and a baggie of miniature mammals in their peculiar extremities—giraffe, elephant, zebra, and so on.

Would you look at these items and say, "*There* is an intelligence I would like to know, would like to have known. We are sensible of the loss"?

We see an article about the show's closing in the Sunday paper: The artists have announced that the entire contents of the gallery will be gathered into a time capsule, just as the title of the show suggested. The time capsule will be buried at Goshen, NY, an active landfill north of the city. The reporter could not say if the glass casket would be empty or occupied; repeated calls have gone unanswered.

———

In our naptime dreams, he disintegrates or he claws his way to the surface of the landfill or he gathers the treasure buried around him—he uses our utensils, rations out the salt and pepper. But this is what we really think: He was put to sleep for the show, he was metaphorically under. In a hundred years, he will wake up in a sweat, literally under, deep in the heat of the fill.

He has lost the thread of his century, but he finds one of the plastic tubes meant to vent gasses, and through it he calls to whatever ears may listen.

THE EXPLORERS CLUB

There is a feeling that we're getting away with something. The exhibit is open to the public, yes, but it's in a club in the toniest part of town, and we find, when we arrive, that we must wait in the foyer to be escorted up to the room on the sixth floor that holds the artist's work.

As we wait, we approach the threshold of a room into which we can see but may not step. It is paneled in the wood of nut or fruit trees, slow-growing trees, the felling of which requires sacrifice. The room is filled with books and tusks, and in the amber light from a floor lamp we can see a man's ankle crossing his knee, a serious newspaper lifted between us. The scene does nothing to dispel the caricatures the name "The Explorer's Club" had conjured: a history of moneyed dilettantes in felt hats; assorted charming social climbers—novelists, doctors, entrepreneurs—looking to plump the virility of their biographies; and seekers unable to distinguish between curiosity and conquest.

But they let us in, and they let in the artist we had come to see. This is the same artist who made The Octagon Room, the same artist who took a large fallen tree from deep in a Pacific Northwest rainforest and transferred it to a city art museum, where he built a massive, mechanized structure so that the tree (and every organism it hosted) might continue its decomposition as if it lay in the forest still. An artist who understands that everything eats something else, and that humans have a special passion for naming and organizing the things they devour.

Our docent arrives, a self-possessed young woman versed in the artist's materials and aims. We suspect, however, when she ushers us into the wood-paneled elevator, that her main function is to keep us from wandering into other rooms, onto other floors, the secrets and privileges of which are for members only.

On the way to the Trophy Room, where the exhibit has been mounted, we pass oil portraits of men in their middle age—notable members, one presumes—as well as photographs of men with one foot on the ribcage of a felled animal or one hand on a mode of transport—prop plane, yak, ship, sled. The only non-white males pictured on the walls are native guides carrying burdens or the reins of beasts of burden. The only women are the docent in front of us and the receptionist downstairs.

We imagine what it must have been to give yourself, at the dawn of the twentieth century, the title "Explorer." How available the world must have felt—still large but no longer frightening, with colonies on every continent and no sea monsters at the edge of the map. "Explorer" was a release valve from an orderly home, a celebration of extremity—it said, *As a subject of study, my home has been exhausted. The data required cannot be found in the vicinity of my habits and my neighbors. To make discoveries, I volunteer to vacate the social contract.* Then they would disappear into a map and return eventually with fertility totems and necklaces made from the claws of lions, the teeth of men.

But when we enter the Trophy Room, our eyes are instantly so busy we forget our bitter critique. Most of the items in the room are old and appear in their original colors: an elk's head in shades of brown, a primitive pot in black and ochre, the silver of swords and rifle barrels, cabinets and furniture of deeply stained wood. And then, the exceptions—there are items scattered throughout the room that appear to be made of stark white plaster. The efforts of our eyes to sort and connect feels like pleasure falling in a mist across our faces and necks. Many of the white objects are spread on a long, substantial table, and the eye registers that they are in the shape of antiquated tools: awl, pulley, coil of rope, lantern, saddlebags, broken-in boots. They are stark replicas of work-bearing tools laid out as if in preparation for an expedition to a futuristic past. Beyond the table, a white boar hangs from the ceiling by its bound feet. There's a white flagpole in the corner, white moth, white campfire on the floor, a cooking pot suspended over it with white sticks. A plush rat-like creature, also white and the size of an eight-year-old child, is pinned on a table as a specimen. Our eyes are hunting and gathering. Our brains are pitched into a colloidal suspension of past and present, respect and irreverence. We are, it occurs to us, explorers in this Trophy Room.

We feel we must be strict with our delight, though. After all, the mere existence of the Trophy Room says, *When members of the club leave home, everything they close their fingers around is a trophy, a victory for them and their kind.* No other taxonomy is required.

The artist has inserted himself into the expeditions, however, and rendered the tools useless and otherworldly white, the quarry comical. This isn't the white of a casual assumption of power, but a cartoon white, an untouchable white, a white that's going to fall to pieces. More importantly, perhaps, the artist suggests a way in, a certain kind of extrapolation that we visitors might take up. We start to follow the lead: We see white objects in the room that aren't actually there—horse bit, crampon, tent. We see the white dust radiating into other rooms, other journeys, into vaults and cabinets with ornate keys. We wonder how the room looked before the artist was invited in. We wonder what happens on the floors from which we are barred. We wonder how many other Trophy Rooms there are in the city and what sorts of stark white objects they might contain. We wonder who might be considered an explorer now and what he might bring back as a trophy. We wonder what sorts of humble tools might now be the means to conquest.

We keep extrapolating on the way back to the elevator, when our time in the Trophy Room has expired. What would the Explorer's Club's version of charity be? Would they hope to teach the next generation how to increase their comfort and dominion at home by taking risks abroad? Perhaps they would host a Future Explorer's Camp for children in the city whose lineage is unlikely to include a club member of any kind. They would scour the foster child rosters, troll the parks and intersections with the worst crime statistics, and hand out fliers and then scholarships.

When camp begins, club members stand the kids in a circle for trust-building exercises, blindfold them and send them into a room, hands forward. They sit them in a circle to tell them about frontiers—"A frontier is a place that needs you to discover it. Your home is a known quantity, it's over. Where can you wield the instruments of measure?" They bring the kids to the Trophy Room to have them study the animal heads on the wall and Explorer's Club flags that have been planted on every continent and even in space. There is a quiz after, but the only question they must get right is: What should people fear more than the gun? Answer: The caliper.

We thank the receptionist sincerely on our way out. We have been given the chance to consider that mounted animal, the gentleman explorer. And consider, too, what frontiers remain—deep space, DMZs, the anaerobic blooms in the oceans, the sites of test bombs, strafing, detonations. Or to consider if the word "frontier" itself is perhaps too slow-moving, might be headed for its own mounting.

That is what the exhibit gave us, but we managed to take a little something, too. Back on the street, we pass addresses that require a household staff—thresholds, archives we will never breach. But in one of our shoulder bags is a pickaxe from the Trophy Room, shedding white plaster dust onto a hairbrush, a whistle, gum wrapped like a pharmaceutical.

It has two satisfying points and a handle that could not have been denied. We wanted this irony in our hands: a tool for exploration, for survival, that, if used, would crumble to dust.

And if we have left something, it is the void where the pickaxe should be. The next visitor might see that void and extrapolate from it. This is what happens when the public is allowed in.

When we get home, we will hang the pickax, the first item on our brand-new trophy wall. Plenty of room for more.

COME IN, IT'S FREE

We were invited to Dublin to curate a robotic art show. Ireland was then the Celtic Tiger, having leapt from its position as one of the poorest nations in the EU, second only to Portugal. We found a city dotted with the cranes and pilings of massive construction projects, flush with biotechs, venture capitalists, software companies, and budget surplus. Flush, too, with immigrants—Eastern Europeans and Asians to wash dishes, sweep streets, and mind babies. Of course the city wanted robots—those slick creatures toward which we're tending or to which we'll cede, according to our folklore.

But conditions did not hold. A year or so later, capital, jobs, citizens, and immigrants began to trickle and then rush out of the country. The government declared bankruptcy. Construction projects halted and then fell back down to earth. Exposed rebar became the ruins of the twenty-first century.

Conditions did not hold—it's a phrase we keep worrying. In retrospect, this experience of Dublin has become a loose collection, gathered under the title of "species drift." The phrase describes random genetic divergence en route to speciation. Finches radiating, forest apes becoming Chimpanzees and Bonobos. Our own purpose there was to wonder about the continuum between art and automation, between human and machine. At the time, we found category instability intriguing.

1. The building we found for the exhibit was a former cathedral, the kind that had displayed fragments of a saint's shin in a glass box, hot under the lights. In a tour of the empty building, the caretaker showed us the vast dirt-floor basement, which, implausibly, contained papier-mâché fire pits, towering faux stone towers, and the prow of an ancient warship. Apparently, the cathedral had fallen on hard times, and when Viking remains had been discovered under the buildings and streets of the neighborhood, entrepreneurs had turned the struggling parish into Dublinia, a "Viking Adventure Center." There had been dioramas, beards and hats with antlers and hairy capes, the "spicy" smell of a Viking village steaming from an unseen vent. But the venture failed, as the Norse rule of Ireland had a thousand years earlier.

In the basement of the cathedral/Dublinia, there was also a mound of black trash bags tagged with what looked like serial numbers.

"These? They're Viking bones."

He pointed to a ripped bag with what, indeed, looked like bones spilling out. They were props as well, yes? No. Cracked bones, fifteen hundred years old. Bone, bone, bone on the dirt basement floor.

2. If pressed, we might say that we were then in our light years. The years that did not require a great deal of negotiation. We liked to say yes to things. We thought that "yes" was a condition that would hold.

3. One piece we chose for the show featured a young female artist who claimed to have constructed a sensitive skin-like substance capable of recording and interpreting human touch. Instead, she crawled inside a box with a computer drawpad for hours and offered the skin of her back to visitors. They used their fingers as styluses and marveled at the shapes they'd drawn appearing on the monitor above the box. A few apprehended the artist's game and some of those smiled, some looked disgusted—human skin, their own skin on it. At one point, a group of pubescent boys lingered around the box. It was unclear whether or not they had figured out the trick, but their laughter was tinted; they may have taken advantage. The artist took a break once they'd moved on, the machine temporarily out of service. We didn't know if she had gotten what or more than she'd hoped for.

4. To the southeast of the former Dublinia, in a neighborhood reminiscent of London (its stately Georgian townhouses owned, historically, by the British ruling elite, which had slowly become—depending on whom you ask—more Irish than British), sat Dublin's Natural History Museum, its collections frozen in the late Victorian age, many of its animals gathered even earlier.

The skunk in the North American section had been sun-bleached to a soft apricot and white. The stretched wings of bats and butterflies had thinned to dust. African mammals bagged out of shape. The rhinoceros, recognizable only by its eponymous nose, looked as if it had swallowed a harem's worth of pillows, flaps of skin peeling like ill-hung wallpaper. Down one entire wall of mammals, a parenthetical echo: *(presumed extinct)*.

We must remind ourselves: this collection does not coalesce. Because it is drifting and we are drifting. What registers, at times, as a fear or a pain or a prickly fascination, is that we do not know what we are drifting toward.

5. We saw in a square what we thought were the most beautiful birds we'd ever seen—large and crisply marked in white, black, and gray. A serious, editorial bird, ready in a moment for a game of billiards or a noble mission. What secrets this island has been keeping, we thought. Irish friends, though, gave a little smirk when we mentioned the birds—"You mean magpies? They're common as pigeons!" And, at once, one bird ate the other, beauty first.

6. At the same time, a well-known artist brought to Dublin a flock of duck decoys outfitted with remote controls, tiny speakers, and microphones so the ducks could emit sound and record their encounters. In a city park, the public was invited to launch the artificial ducks into a large pond so that they might communicate with the flesh and feather ducks. This was meant as an experiment in how biological ducks respond

to robotic ducks ostensibly "speaking their language." An experiment, too, in how people, operating the robotic ducks remotely, respond to having a duck avatar. Only, for the most part, the ducks didn't work. And when a child actually drove her duck across the pond and got it to squawk, the biological ducks didn't pause or twitch. It was as if they'd been living with or negotiating around mechanized versions of themselves since they'd genetically drifted into the category *duck*.

The richest moment, though, came when the artist took one of the ducks to a radio interview and forgot it in the cab. Assistants called all over the city to try to locate it. That duck was without a homing device, out of range of its remote control, riding a cab through the city. It was never found; it may be riding still, recording.

7. After a trickle of visitors the first morning of the three-day show, we went with volunteers and artists out into the streets with fliers. People were often kind, inquisitive: *A robotic art show, what's that, then? Here in Dublin, isn't that something? And where are you from, love?*

One artist took his piece to a nearby market to attract more visitors. He had made a robot rover the size of a tricycle designed to be driven by a Madagascar Hissing Cockroach. Perched on a trackball, the insect served as the robot's CPU. It drove around the market and then back to the hall like a Pied Piper of future disaster: cockroaches and rovers, people following in undifferentiated hoards.

Outside the back door of the exhibit space, the huffers hung out. They did what they could afford, blisters around their mouths and noses, older scabs up the undersides of their arms. There was a leader, it seemed, with a girl and a baby. He twitched from one corner to the next and back again in a parody of a male bird returning to the nest.

The huffers took fliers, flicked their eyes around the page. *It's free?* Later, the same at the door, craning their necks: *It's free?* But inside, they lasted only minutes, ricocheting like birds caught indoors—up the stairwell, an erratic loop through the hall, then down the back stairs, where visitors encountered the only humanoid robot in the show. A metal skeleton, white plastic eye exposed, cables running like ligaments throughout, it was a collision of the futuristic and old-fashioned manual labor. People could work in concert on a system of eight levers positioned around the room to make each joint bend or limb swing. Visitors made it wave hello, made it smack its forehead, made it drag its arms like an ape, and then left, exhausted with the effort. After a few moments watching, the huffers left, too, without trying the levers. It was impossible to deny how hard they already worked.

We watched the leader on and off for the three days of the show—his speed, his flock, their open economy. We knew we were watching their cells reorganizing; we think they knew that, too. But something was nipping at our dendrites, as well, a knowledge we could only later try to collect: that every living thing is drifting between species or already extinct.

This is not a conclusion:

It occurs to us that we could have taken a Viking bone from the basement as the caretaker led us out. We regret, at times, that we did not. We might have smuggled it home in our suitcase: one abused clavicle wrapped in a hostel towel and tucked under our dirty clothes. An old bone in the New World. It would have been buried along with us and our things when our apartment building goes under. Another mystery for future archeologists, be they robot, insect, or primate.

And, because there is no ending, because we don't know the ending:

On our way home, we held hands as the plane took off and again when it touched down. We always do.

YEAR 5

After the baby was born, they moved us to a room that coincidentally had a view of the city and the tidal river. It was still dark and so what we saw were lights stacked ill-advisedly high, with a black trough cut next to them. What we saw were the two dark eyes and the hair swirl of a creature grave and new.

When night fell again, one of us had to leave. (Families could stay together if they had purchased a private room, but that was on another floor, another city.) Strangely, two of us remained. Nurses entered and left through the night. One nurse said, "If you don't put that baby down, it's going to get attached to you."

GONE

I read an article about the exhibit before I saw it. The critic was charmed—he found the artist not broody or particularly deep, but infused with a joy that created its own profundity. Yes, I thought, I would like to see that, I would like some profound joy.

Still, I went skeptical. I wasn't sure that I would take to its compositional elements—something about footage of cavorting sheep in layered projections, animated neon squiggles, a lullaby playing in the background. I wondered, too, if the reviewer was smitten in part because the artist was Swiss and her name was Pipilotti and the exhibit involved the aforementioned sheep on hilltops. She might as well be Heidi.

I didn't anticipate how my senses would be commandeered. The room was dark and filled with loose light alleys of curtains shifting in the slightest current. Each row of curtains showed a different angle on the sheep—a middle-distant shot of a herd cresting a hill; a camera down in the grass, nuzzled by a succession of whiskered lips; an aerial view of sheep milling below, then jolting together down a gentle valley. The curtains were so transparent I could see through one projection to the next and the next, and walk right into the herd. Sheep at a distance. Sheep right up front, swallowing my hand. The light on the open hills was munificent; the sun shafts in the dark room angled down, right into my eye. And the music, plunk-plunking the back of my neck, perfectly evoked an endangered serenity—the music of everyone's and no one's childhood.

I had learned in the previous months something about being commandeered. I had, in fact, brought the commander, my infant, to the show, but he was with his father in another room. For once in what seemed like days, maybe months, he was not touching me. He was an impression on the skin, a cry stuck in my head that every sound at every pitch seemed to mimic. I closed my eyes and his face and nothing else floated in front of me. He had been my mind since he was born—not *in* or *on*, but the whole of my mind. Like the apparently normal woman I'd read of who was found, in an unrelated test, to have a thin smear of brain around the perimeter of her skull and a great empty bubble in the middle; I had the bubble, filled with child, without the smear.

This was what it was like, for me, to have a baby, a baby in the next room with his father: vacant and present, and present and present; right precisely there, and gone, too.

———

But under the influence of this room, he was next to my mind and we were both floating in the music of the universal nursery.

I am embarrassed to say "and then something happened," but it did. One of the airy curtains wafted and grazed the back of my head and left shoulder, the kind of touch that releases—a mother's touch, my mother the sheep, or the touch of someone I didn't know I wanted until the moment of contact, when a life together sprang into the mind. I gave myself over completely to the piece. I had been holding something back, as if the special, private thing I keep for myself is an unwitting clench. I let go and floated loose-limbed and faceless into the work.

I was a projection into the projections, a handful of photons tossed into the air. Even the neon squiggles now seemed exactly right, forms that existed between hills, eyes, and cells. We were atomized: mote, sunspot, plant fluff, sheep breath, shoulder, plunk plunk. What can a body do to stay bodiless for just a moment more?

Pipilotti's room suspended me. I was gone and grateful, and then I came back, where my infant waited next door, and was grateful for that, too. I walked into the next room.

WITHOUT ATTRIBUTION

A car on the highway is a thought nurtured by the blurred landscape. I was moving inside of this swift thought with the stereo silent and my passengers—one grown and one infant boy—asleep for just these few moments out of the day. Part of my mind was tracking the lines of the road, the bumpers, the wind against the broadside of the car; part of it was in the backseat resting against a pillow, picking up pieces of the future and setting them back down again.

Then I saw a cluster of towering spotlights in the highway median. I immediately thought "art," though I can't say why. They could simply have been floodlights for nighttime construction, or even lights for a film crew shooting a road scene. But the lights looked like descriptions of themselves, like you were supposed to notice that they were lights before seeing what they were lighting. They were closer together than one would expect. And there was the sense of a hand lingering over the spotlight's placement, authorship. As how, under a confluence of chiseled mountain, tree, and lake, an atheist might slip and think *God*. It seemed as if a mind had thought these spotlights into being, and so my mind reflexively thought of that mind.

It was an invitation that mind issued, and I loved the feeling of responding to it—*Okay, let's go*—almost like a romance. It was daylight and the lights were not on—or at least not visible—but before flashing by at a speed I hoped was not worth a trooper's time, I saw that they were pointed not at the highway but at the land on the opposite side of the road, a field of corn planted on a hill sloping gently up and flanked by trees. The object of five magnificent spotlights was simply this: a field of corn.

The richness made my breath catch. Flying down the highway, the landscape like a radio between stations, we are on our way and movement feels famous—the eye, the camera follows us. And then suddenly, For Your Consideration: corn as bully crop, corn as rows of nostalgia, corn as what is most fecund and simple and rabid about America. The spotlights said, Here is celebrity, here is event. You on the highway are the white noise. You could do worse than to wait and watch, the piece suggests, while knowing that you won't. There is no pause. You will take along only a flash of this ordinary, famous sight.

I hoped this was a series and in a month, a year, I would look down and find a specimen dome over a weed coming up through the sidewalk.

They might, after all, have been construction floodlights. It was summer and every highway in the country was being chewed up and frosted smooth. But I decided it was the best art I'd seen in a long time.

OUTLAWS AND CITIZENS

We had been meaning to go for so long, out of the city and up to their studio, where we heard the structure was constantly being built. Bamboo lashed to more bamboo starting up into the sky unsteadily, without a plan or an end, accreting by the whim of visitors who were invited to drop by, clamber up into the network of sticks and add a new branch, a next step. You could sway at the end of a stick, perched over nothing—like so many explorers at the lips of canyons, drawing the map as they went along.

We imagined the structure as looking alive, creeping forward or upward—an organism—in the inevitable time-lapse film. And what would be the upper limit? How high was too high? It sounded dangerous and fun. The sort of thing that dangerous and fun people would make a point not to miss. Perhaps, increasingly, the sort of thing that only happened once a waiver had been signed or in desert states where the laws of nature were terribly apparent but the laws of man could be negotiated.

Our minds delighted in the idea: We climbed and tested the give of various branches with our feet. We learned
the names of knots and felt a little thrill when the ground
disappeared in a mist. It was likely we would have been
changed by the experience. Often, when our bodies try
something new, our minds are made unbalanced and sur-
prisable. Open. But to leave the city, even for a thirty-minute
drive, we felt we would have to take everything we might
possibly need, even the things we couldn't anticipate. Thus
we had difficulty overcoming inertia; we simply couldn't
get ourselves moving. Our bodies sweated out the late
summer heat on our apartment floors, weak fans trained
at our heads.

The next thing we knew, the artists had been invited to build
a version of the bamboo structure on the roof of the city's
museum. It's a public museum in every sense, an institution
with ancient sculptures and paintings that make popular
postcards, and we hadn't been in years. The idea that this
renegade structure was now growing on its roof was enough
to get us moving. Besides, we would never otherwise have
access to the museum's roof.

Next to gardens, roofs are the most elusive and coveted
property in the city. They are, perhaps, the city's frontier.
Laws that govern the commons somehow do not apply to
city rooftops. It is a most severely defined patch of freedom.

When we exited the elevator, we saw a bamboo walkway
rising up, turning corners, and becoming engulfed in more
bamboo. It was more an airy sidewalk than an emergent

structure. From a distance, it could almost have been the entrance to a safari-themed amusement ride.

We could not walk up into it with sandals on.

We couldn't walk up with small children.

Not without signing a clipboard full of papers.

In fact, we could not walk up at all. Visitors were only allowed to ascend in a guided tour, select time slots offered online days in advance.

We could walk among the bamboo structures that formed its base, though, and look up through the branches and catch sight of the visitors' skirts and shorts puffing in the breeze. Along the perimeter, they had installed fencing to prevent jumpers and fallers, we supposed, and through it we could glimpse crowds in the park below reshuffling, as if they were test subjects entering and exiting affiliate groups.

At either end of the roof was a bar, servers in crisp white selling cocktails and Northern European beers at black-tie prices.

This was not *our* sculpture. In our minds, we were up in the structure on the artists' own property, without waitlists or guided tours or demands for close-toed shoes. We are climbing up, up and up, until we're at the top, creating the next foothold ourselves. On the roof, we wanted something that was meant for many only for ourselves. Only for myself. I'm up there, facing the empty prairie, behind me barbed wire and cultural treasures, behind me all the entanglements of citizenship, the sharing of bowls and water and air. As if "I" were a clean slate, a best hope. As if, to make way for "I," "we" had to be kicked back down.

———

In the end, we stayed up on the roof for a long time. The structure was very beautiful—patterns in the tightly fitted bamboo, pops of color in the slender lashings. Eventually, we plopped down, spread our legs out in front of us, and stared up into the branches. We weren't the only ones: a picnicking spirit prevailed. We produced food from pockets and bags, wrangled babies, pulled at bottles of beer, called to strangers. We felt oddly light, surrounded by so much bamboo at so many angles. We were surprised how comfortably we settled in, how freely we laughed.

And I, that little spindle behaving unaccountably out in the world—she is swaddled with other "I"s, not a danger to herself or others.

YEAR 6

For the first year after the birth, we acted as if the laws that governed us formerly had been vacated. We ate bloody hamburgers, collected bulging bags of takeout containers, made $200 trips to infant retailers where we paid to allay fears we hadn't yet entertained. We took cabs, did not wash and reuse our Ziploc bags. We made ourselves as comfortable as we could. If it would have given us a few more hours of rest, we would have melted a tower of plastic, poured battery acid into a reservoir, scraped back the top of a mountain looking for something to burn. Because nobody knew the difficulty of the project we'd undertaken. No one but the other 130 million people who had given birth that year or any other.

For a year, it was as if we were floating on a houseboat in fog, and we didn't wonder that we did not see land or another human being, that we could not even step on deck to gulp down some salt air. We realized one day that we had not even looked at one another during this time, but had instead been operating as separate parts of a life-support mechanism.

We began, then, to look at one another for a few seconds at a time, to build up our tolerance. We had to train to rejoin the human race—

acknowledge the speech of others, prop our eyes open as waves of people passed on the sidewalk, tune the radio occasionally to the news. Our mouths had practiced language for many years, and, even though they were rusty, we used them to form these words: we are not exempt, we are in it, we are in it, we are in it, we are in it, we are in it.

BACK ROOMS

The youngest among us learned early and absolutely not to touch the art, but we don't know sometimes how he resists— cotton candy–colored rabbits with phalluses; a statue of a dog having a bowel movement on the sidewalk; parachute blown open when an industrial fan roars to life; watchworks bringing a pig, a clown, a politician to life; square of turf with a tiny figure holding a nearly invisible thread leading to a wee kite, far above its head.

We can see him thinking how good that figure would feel in his hand, how the kite would follow him, and how, in possession of such tininess, he himself could feel both big and small. He was invited to feel these things by the artists who, wittingly or not, in galleries tricked up like rarified toy stores, trigger an itch in our fingers. Art has depended on covetousness and elusiveness for a long time. If we had a great deal of money (and no worries about depreciation), we could get to know it with our hands;

otherwise, art is nearly always literally and figuratively out of reach.

As we burn through our own store of willpower, we say to him, "Whatever you do, don't touch." Wars must rage inside his mind, and in a war things die. We teach him to be proud of the dark patches spreading in his brain. We teach him to ingest the protocol: you chase after a bit of magic, thwart yourself (in the manner of serfs and parishioners), then take in what you can from a distance and let it ricochet behind your eyes. However, here's a secret we know that he may come to appreciate: Behind your eyes is where the art resides. Whatever your eyes take is yours.

The guards are convinced that he will touch; they rush over, hover or admonish. But he will not. He is eager to prove himself without reminder and stung by their lack of trust. He would like them to recognize that he's in the know, part of the ruling oligarchy, the grown world. He has added "I won't!" and "I wasn't going to!" to his two-year-old lexicon. He shakes his finger, shakes his head.

"He won't," we tell the guards. "He wasn't going to."

We set off one day with a list of galleries we'd like to see, boxes to check off, carrying light provisions, pushing or prodding children, hoping something would happen to us. We didn't know what; we figured we'd know when it happened.

The first gallery played advertisements collaged into frenetic videos that might have imperiled an epileptic. The children barely glanced at the walls; instead, they danced as if in a discotheque, and our only pleasure was their pleasure.

The second gallery was dimly lit save for a red button on the wall, from which ran wires to loosely constructed plywood boxes, one each on three walls of the main room, another by the entrance, a few more in a small back room. We made sure that what was implied, what had been triggered in us (*red button—push!*), was, in fact, allowed: *Go ahead, push the red button!* Then we lifted the youngest one, let him push it, and congratulated ourselves on being the curators of his delight.

The box closest to the button began whirring, clicking, and flashing. A black-and-white film projected onto the one blank wall: we saw an exterior shot of a small trailer in a scrub desert, then the interior, and repeat. We put it together that the machinations in the box were creating the film, and we tried to see between the slats of the box how the illusion was made. The gaps were big enough to imply that we might glimpse the miniature sets inside, but small enough to obscure our view.

We were supposed to want to see in and then be frustrated. And we did and we were. None more so than the youngest, who had no interest in the film, only in the boxes alive with theoretical activity, a world without him. Each box switched on in turn, and by the fourth box, after requesting our intercession (*Help me see inside! Why can't you help me?*), he gave up and asked to be put down. He ran a few laps through the projections and then came to an abrupt halt in front of a curtained archway that led, presumably, to a back office. He looked to us, then back at the curtain. He edged closer. Looked to us, curtain, us, his curiosity irrevocably transferred.

We continued with our list, cut a swath through the city from west to east, the vintage of gentrification getting fresher, the real estate prices rising, the art employing increasingly more neon and mirrors. We stood in places that had been arranged for our viewing. But, in truth, we were mostly watching what the youngest of us was watching. We had never until that day noticed all of the darkened doors, the forbidden spaces of the galleries. A curtained doorway, a dim hall, doors that we (but not he) knew led to backrooms, washrooms, closets, circuit breakers. In each gallery, at each dark space and closed door, the youngest of us stopped and pointed with grave desire, with reverence. He turned on us eyes full of sentences. *Can I go back there? We've never even been here before. Come, come. Come, come, come!*

This is what happened to us that day: We realized that he had taken in the lesson of the whirring boxes more completely than we had, and more completely than we could have imagined: reality was being composed in the spaces to which we had no access. He wanted into the back rooms, the rooms that ran the whole show, that lit the lights. That was where he had work to do.

NOW, BY WHICH WE MEAN THEN, BY WHICH WE MEAN SOON, AND AGAIN

Throughout the room were large glass vitrines containing items—an engine block, the wing of a bomber, miniature wooden tugs and tankers—that looked dragged from a mudslide or a shallow grave. The hem of a white dress was nearly buried in shards of glass. A typewriter sat muddy on a folding chair, keys akimbo and skewered by branches. A thorn bush caught a flood-swollen book. They were artifacts, meant to testify to the disaster they'd survived. The vitrines implied a studious approach, but the items seemed so attended to, and with such a needful eye, that the room was more reliquary than laboratory.

The show was called Next Year in Jerusalem. The Passover salute capturing the diaspora, the fervent or wistful or rote wish for unification in the holy land.

But in this room, "Next Year in Jerusalem" took on a new meaning. Were we looking at the tragedies that would, by next year, have befallen that riven city? Were we looking at artifacts from the future, or had we, ourselves, stepped out of time? The reams of ruined film, the mangled chairs, the letters plowed under and dug out. "Artifacts from the future" was an impossible assemblage of words made possible because there we were, with our feet on the floor. Looking at a forest of blighted branches, the corroded hull of a submarine, we experienced the curious sensation of nostalgia for future losses. The youngest among us studied the ruined white dress for longer than his attention span should have allowed. He left pea-sized fingerprints on the glass—little ridges of oil and epithelium.

In the center of the room was a steel bunker with a hulking door on one side and another on the end, both propped open. They looked so heavy as to suggest they would never be moved again. Through the narrow openings we could see that the artist had suspended a row of screens; on each one, blown up large, was a photograph in sepia tones—his childhood memories hung from great hooks. We could glimpse only a few through the openings. They were peaceful, ominous: a young man in lederhosen on what was either mountain or rubble, his arm raised straight in front of him; the neat and narrow street of a small town with an incongruously broken wall. It was Germany, of course, and how could we not all think the same thoughts nearly at once: six million, citizen executioners. The steel walls, they were not to protect the memories but to protect us from the images we couldn't see.

———

Next year in Jerusalem.

We will be sifting through the wreckage. The past will come up through the ground.

He placed us in a moment of study between disasters and then let us know how empty the pretense of containment—the oversized glass vitrines, the steel bunker. Though we might unearth and collect and display, though we might mill about in clothes with all of their buttons and an artfully frayed hem, though we might have been asked to leave a stroller at the door so as not to mar the staging, we are merely *between* the kinds of histories that eat the paint from your hull, that drop the sparrows from the sky. They are waiting for us on either end.

Next year in Jerusalem, glass will have returned to sand. Next year, now will be then, just as then has been pulled through now again and again. We were looking at tomorrow's history: yet-to-be-exploded ordnance washed up on the beach. *Now* is a disaster we have not yet framed.

Afterward, we could not agree: some of us disliked the bigness of it, the right words there being "grandiosity," "melodrama"—ruins! Present and eternal conflict! Some of us said, yes, that is so, it was very German. But some of us said, Perhaps that was the point, there being no way to escape your past. Others said they did not want to go to church and worship holy objects. One was put off by the crowd. A few of us were too busy not knowing where to put our feet, not sure where the present was, spooked to think apocalypse might not come all at once. Through what will we be dragged in the coming days, months? Surely something that will warp or cling or peel.

————

Six months later, plus or minus one or two of us, we return to the address. It's purportedly the same building, the same gallery, but it's not now the space it was.

The entryway is different, the walls have been moved—have they really been *moved?*—and the whole huge space has been filled with serpentine steel walls curving toward the ceiling. We enter a hallway of graceful steel that angles toward us in one spot, and then bends away in another, opens into a den and then closes again into a passageway. It goes on and on, turns corners, narrows. We no longer know where we are; some of us have disappeared around a bend. We swallow a touch of panic at the back of our throats before we are released into the room we entered.

There is a similar structure on the other side of the room. We have to think for a moment if we want to enter it and leave the gallery, the city, and all sense of context again.

As we exit the second structure, a guard animates in the presence of the youngest of us, just a baby, really. They learn each other's names, the guard amazed when the baby speaks. The guard makes a threatening noise, fingers turning into claws, and the baby shrieks and runs away and then back. It is a pantomime with infinitely rotating players, but the baby seems particularly fond of this player, the guard, Ken. They repeat the play, again and again.

A short while later, after we've migrated to a different part of the room, the baby calls for him, "More Ken, more Ken!" He runs into one of the steel labyrinths shouting, "More

Ken," and one of us runs after. We are all amused by the sudden attachments of children.

We leave having absorbed a new sense of scale—the steel so imposing and yet so close to our skin. We're pleased with the sensations settling in, having felt ourselves lost inside massiveness and solidity and then led safely out again. With our feet back on the sidewalk, though, the then begins pulling through the now. From the outside, we see that this *is* the same building as six months before, and we have an unbidden thought: Why would a stranger give a stranger-child so much of his energy? What if the guard had been left alone with him? What if children move inexorably toward what will wound them? What if we cannot see the danger?

This is history large and small, after all: people who could not see the danger. Preoccupied with the lift and drag of each moment—overdrawn account, minor fatigue, an occasional surge of excitement, dark feelings that blot out a day, holes in our pockets through which coins and cough drops and directions tend to slip—we have forgotten what we learned just six months before: that now is a disaster we have not yet framed. We will have to suspect more and sooner in the future. This time next year, you will not know us.

CRIME IS DOWN ALL OVER

One of our fathers says it's time to lay in provisions. At least a month's worth. His voice has traveled out of the woods a long way. The way, he has said, we must travel if anything happens: bomb, drone, wave, fire, a great poisoning of the well. Humans testing their species in this largest of North American cities. We are not wasps, he says, built for the hive. *Get in the car and don't look back.*

His garage is larger than his living space. Bundles of meticulously coiled nylon rope in the rafters, a society of tools below. There is more than one of everything—hat, life vest, can of stew—at least a breeding pair. The case of pilaf, when we visit, has gone off.

The two of us, we are unafraid. We have chosen density and signed the social contract. We offer ourselves like a gift to the universe. We press cell phones to our ears, allow cameras throughout the city to capture our comings and goings. Our first-aid kit has been pilfered and not restocked. We do not have chlorine tablets, a fire ladder, or waterproof matches, we do not kick the car tires. We have not saved, do not save, will not be saved. On an afternoon drive, we picnic happily among the plastic periscopes of a seeded landfill.

But the father's phone calls persist and the idea of storage captures our fancy—non-perishables as art. We draw plans for the shelter we would build if we thought we needed sheltering: there would be lead walls and a billiard room, an infinity pool—why not? Then, in caricature or homage, we work for weeks in the hours after the baby is asleep, marking grains of rice, barely speaking. We inscribe a tiny segment of the architectural lines on each grain. Brown rice because it is more nutritious, at least a month's worth.

We begin in the hallway (that placeless place, the way out) and affix grain after grain with wheat paste, until the walls are covered. We sit back on our haunches to appraise and we are pleased. All those tiny lines, the shelter an open secret. In the low light of the hallway, you wouldn't know. Maybe it's wallpaper, maybe stucco, maybe a fungus.

You really shouldn't be riding the subway anymore. That's how they're going to get you; that's how they're going to bring the city down.

Our upstairs neighbor has come for a visit—no, she has come to ask about a whir in her floorboards/our ceiling. She didn't want to say anything, really it's no big deal, she begins, and then trails off. She's staring at the wall. The neighbor leans toward its nubby surface and then looks at us. That is to say, she takes us in.

An art project, we say. Art project. We move toward each other and link hands, as if our proximity might comfort her—the appearance of benign domesticity.

We see in her eyes a sudden tabulation of the trust we must daily offer, uncountable if we'd like to think beyond our survival. She has passed us many times in the stairwell; we say enough to facilitate a pleasant feeling and then swift forgetting. But we haven't been out in days. We notice, now, the smell of trash hard upon us, and we notice her noticing that she's standing in our space, her back to the door. The disorder of our bookshelves could conceal almost anything. Our walls are just below her walls and help to hold her up. We see her recalibrating to a new set of threats.

The whir, she says, is not so bad. No really, don't worry.

The hallway dampens the noise of the closing door. And in the persistent quiet of the coming days, we hear her footsteps from one end of our ceiling to the other. Her muffled voice funneled into a cell phone.

Would you like me to get you a shotgun? Everyone should have one. Just in case.

We have many walls to go, but we take a little rest, lie flat on the floor while the baby stumbles between us. If the walls shake down now, we will be surrounded. Plaster, layers of lead and acrylic paint, horsehair and sawdust stuffed into the hollows of the old apartment walls. But also rice grains, each bearing a line that might connect to another line. We will eat them by the millions to survive.

LAMARCKIAN EVOLUTION

Once upon a time, a long time from now, there are monkeys who feed at ancient landfills. They swallow the parts they need to wire or pad or decorate their bodies—foam fill, glass beads, plastic baby bottles, spiral phone cords (the kind that, for a brief time, teenage girls wrapped obsessively around their fingers), sequined upholstery fabric, pumps to fill and pumps to empty. They lap at the silicone they need to coat their sockets and cavities. They are both tender and territorial with one another. They do as their parents taught: clean the worst of the garbage from their white fur, pluck rebar and fiberglass and staples from each other's paws. One pauses, considers a string of plastic beads, adds it to his haunch. Their babies, they are pleased to note, are born part flesh, part rubber, wire, and watchworks.

This is what we saw when we walked into the gallery: tableaux of these monkeys, their fur incompletely stretched over their bodies, not quite covering their jaws or joints.

Some creatures' bellies or trachea were entirely exposed or covered with translucent domes or replaced with upholstery that looked scavenged from a bordello. Their breasts, genitals, and mouths looked fancy and painful. But they were also bubbling with what might have been tumors. Spray insulation frothed from the gaps in their fur. They didn't seem to see us or need us; they were carrying on with their relationships, a nuzzle here, a puncture wound there. And those familiar items—tube, cord, drinking straw—seemed both to be holding them up and making them terminally ill. They had loped back through time on their composite limbs to hold very still for us.

In our group in the gallery, there were several babies, all walking and talking, a few nursing still, the oldest among them not yet three.

The babies circled the groups of monkeys holding their poses, asked to be held up so that they might peer more closely at their faces, their rumps, and their bellies full of treasure. One said, "I don't like this," then looked and looked and said, "I like this." Then they found a darkened room in the back that was showing a stop-motion film with a calliope soundtrack. The babies filed in of their own accord and, as if by agreement, felt their way to the bench in the center of the room and crawled up on it. The monkeys moved jerkily, enacting the story of a couple in their glittering, dry ice cave. They had a dog that grew weak and was eaten. They had silent rivalries and fantasies about their own goodness. They had vicious sex and then gestated a monkey child. When it came to term, the mother slit her own belly with a sharp fingernail and the baby slid out in a cascade of iridescent glass beads. The final shot was of a clear plastic monkey breast filling with milk and the baby's mouth working toward it.

When the end of the film played, the babies said, "Mommy's milk," sternly at first, like a demand or even a reprimand. The film looped and they murmured, "Mother." It looped again and they remembered their mothers as if they were something that had happened to the babies long ago. "Mother," they felt the word with their mouths. "Mommy...Mama." It began to dissolve on their tongues like a tuft of cotton candy. "Ma...mmm," they said, smiling, wistful. They reached for each other's hands, hugged, tried to push one another from the bench. The oldest leaned over to the youngest and said "I love you" in a stage whisper. The movie began anew every six minutes, and the babies sat there in the dark a long time.

We took turns peeking through the heavy velvet curtains at the doorway to make sure no child was being devoured. We wondered if we had swallowed the things we needed, if we had swallowed the things they needed and passed them along. We wondered what would happen if we left. How long would they sit with the glistening, mutated monkeys in the dark? How long would they hold hands, turn and offer each other pathogens on their wet lips? How long would it take them to realize they were on their own?

YEAR 7

When we were young, we (in truth, one of us, but in greater truth, a whole army of children) thought it was a given that the world would end in our lifetime. We spent a lot of time draped over the arm of a pine tree trying to work out the logistics—how would we know the Rapture was beginning, how could we be sure that a disqualifying thought would not streak across our minds in that unforeseen moment? Are we right with God now…now…now? Our chest cavities caught and warmed. The corners of our mouths turned up with what one might read as a deep and secret pleasure or as the measure of a sociopath.

Being certain of apocalypse meant that no story had to be finished, no difficulty endured, no relationship mended or even understood; a way of being that was both thrilling and lazy. And this sweet world— the thicket of thimble berries stumbled upon, the sweaty hair of our friends laid in our laps, stalk of rhubarb mashed into a bowl of sugar, our anaerobic wonder when, at twilight, the light leached from the sky—we sold it out quick.

People have been in love with vacating their lives for at least as long as they have been recording them. But one story of the twentieth century could be told entirely in terms of the byproducts that will persist beyond our children and our children's children, beyond even human ability to understand time. Stronium, DDT, arsenic, CO_2, diapers, hexachlorobenzene, Styrofoam, toxaphene, irradiated waste. A million years, ten million. Peak oil, water wars, dead oceans. Environments "rendered inhospitable to human life." These are excellent stories to skip out on. If we could but conjure again that quaint narcissism, the one that says the world will end because we can't see beyond tomorrow.

We get a plastic container full of plastic animals for our child—"Jungle Toob!"—and he loves them. Loves them. They feature in every project, every trip, every day. We have made him fall for animals that will not survive his lifetime. We tell him we will visit the jungles of Zimbabwe someday, step quietly through the mountain fauna until we meet a gorilla and speak with him, just as we've practiced. That is the best many animals can hope for—to be the object of human fantasy, the subject of an animated movie.

In the "Gorilla Encounter" at the zoo, we whisk him past the photographs of severed gorilla hands and feet, their heads on sticks. We would like to find a way to look this straight in the face, but we've had so little practice.

SHE CAME BACK

The artist has been away. We know this as soon as we walk in. Not just away from us, but away from humans. She made a home someplace other than Earth. An outpost.

She must have been gone a long time. We can tell because she took with her our earthly things—water bottles, mint tins, measuring cups, compasses, playing cards, squirt bottles, paper clips, little plastic monkeys from a barrel—and kept them away long enough that they lost their labels and their function, and then brought them right back.

On the sparest balsam racks filling the sizeable room, our things are displayed with precision, like grouped with like. She has arranged them as a study of the species, as if she, herself, had forgotten her context and can now handle it only with calipers. Whitewashed milk cartons are clustered high and thick; small discs lined up according to size; concrete molds of mice, tails broken on the journey back. Some items seem to have been coated in plaster, like water bottles, notebooks, and boxes that likely held all manner of carbohydrate—cereal, cracker, partially boiled rice, and corn syrup–coated corn. We can only guess; no hint of the objects' first function remains. They are outlines of themselves, as if they—or we—are rumors heard fourth-hand.

We're not prepared for this, we would not choose it, to be the objects of study, to give up labels and the colloquial names for things. Would we have come if we'd known how blank and unsteady she would turn us? We don't want milk so much as the picture of the split-rail-fenced farm on the package, the cow that looks us in the eye with its own very large, friendly eye, and is happy to whiten our cereal. We don't want water so much as we want the signs of endless water: in the Jiffy Mart a wall of chilled, clear-blue bottles. The brand's same tasteful suggestion of a wave propagating across a warehouse, big rig, billboard, drink dispenser, and label picked nervously to ribbons.

The thing is, our things look lovely without us, lined up for study. They do not miss us. So the missing falls to us, and it's a heavy burden.

We can barely move our bodies from place to place; are we also expected to become wise? She asks us to imagine what we are without the backdrop that floods our passive vision. We look at the street sign but we see without seeing the telephone pole, meter box, padlock, curb, blackened gum on the concrete in an inverse constellation, four makes of cars, bumper stickers, brand names circling tires, litter, litter, litter, garbage can, dry cleaner with five Asian lady posters, man with a child, presumably his own, child with

Buzz Lightyear socks and a forearm bruise, woman stooping over a broken-toothed dog, two teenagers in flammable pants moving fast.

Erase it.

Everything but the juice box that was next to, not in, the trashcan, and is now dipped in plaster.

Now: imagine an American dollar store in the early nineties, a miniature baby bottle with a clear plastic strip along the side. When you tip the bottle up, a fabricated bubble moves along the strip from the top to the bottom, where "Made in China" is stamped.

Imagine working in a factory that makes items for a culture entirely unknown to us, items for which we have no reference. We would spend our finite time, the efforts of a body that wears out, on filling up boxes with things that some days seem frivolous, some days sinister. Who could want this hollow and bent section of plastic, and in such violent colors? We would have forgiven her if she hadn't wanted to return.

Upstairs, in a darkened room, she had rebuilt a structure she must have used on her outpost. When we saw it, we knew that coming back was probably not obligatory or accidental—she had missed her home. The structure was part spaceship, part nest, part hippocampus. Two-by-fours framed the loose suggestion of a sphere. In lieu of walls, she had hung a lattice of picture postcards: lush greens merging into tidal blues, blues into molten lava, into turned fields.

The Earth is so beautiful it makes the backs of our throats burn. Wherever she went, it was not as beautiful, otherwise the new place would have made her forget the old. Leaf and blueberry, sunset and beetle, fireweed, jellyfish, honeycomb, tidal pool, plum ripe to splitting.

Everything we didn't make, that dies and disappears.

At the door, we take a sheet that promises to tell us more. But her biography makes no mention of her missing years, how she survived re-entry into our atmosphere. What it was like to be, for a time, not a citizen, not one of a species.

We think maybe time works differently out there. Decades pass for her in a star field, and when she comes back less than a season has turned on Earth. She may be the fourth generation of herself, but back home, she is understood as Sarah, Sarah still.

Or maybe we're wrong, and she never left. It's easy to be wrong these days; a fact becomes mostly false between swallows. Do you remember that you are swallowing? Do you know how fast we will forget our planet?

THE WELL

The well is poisoned, he says on the phone one week; then, another week, *It's drying up.*

The story, the beloved story, used to be that under our wilderness—so wild it was unlocatable on any map—was an aquifer deep and pure. It was ours and we drank from the ground with a straw.

Now, when we visit him, it is during the thick and showy summer months, the woods full of breezes and animated green. He points out a property a few miles up the road with oozing tanks, junked cars and trailers, and, between them, scabby animals tied to stakes. He is sure the owners have poisoned the ground and the ground has poisoned the water. He will not have it tested, though, preferring his fear to a number of parts-per-million.

At the well house, he shows us the slackened flow. *Too many people,* he says, *are tapping into it.* Ours was not the only straw.

———

Home again, we take a long subway ride from our borough to the next to see a group art show called "Heat Island," a term meant to describe the urban center as heat trap and sink. Raw sunlight falls on concrete, steel, and brick, where it pools and breeds; heat churns, too, from within—motors, lights, cars, appliances stacked into the sky, an air conditioner dripping from every other window. The heat of millions of animals compounding without release.

We admit we are afraid of heat; we were not raised to be trapped. We throw our windows open all winter. We have the available shade mapped for the time of year, the time of day. The city is unable to breathe and we don't know how to make lungs—that thought sits on us leadenly. We have come to Heat Island to become fascinated by the ways we can't help ourselves.

A wall of mirrored bricks is the first piece we see. And then construction materials—cinderblock, drywall, insulation—piled in a heap by another artist. Then a whimsically large fan trained at a whimsically large couch on a platform a few feet from the ground. There are three drums on which we're invited to pound. Further, a few monotonous oil paintings of housing project exteriors, and a second heap of building materials by a *different* artist, this one with a blank canvas draped over one side.

We're won over by the scale of the couch and fan, and we like the intentional monotony of the paintings. But we feel like a finicky Goldilocks—this piece is too obvious, this one is too cute, too lazy, too preachy, too pretty. One over and one under-determined. Nothing is just right. Or we are not right for them. The corners of our lips fall until our mouths are flat lines, then fall further. Our eyes have less radiance than the photographs of gasoline puddles.

We had wanted to see something capacious, an invitation for the mind to dig into the body's conundrums. None of the works feel big enough to crawl into, as when early humans sought shelter in caves but then carefully mixed rust and ochre paints and brought the danger inside, their thumb tips tracing haunch and horn. We wanted to crawl into the Heat Island or invite it inside, the difference between the two perhaps negligible in the end.

We leave and notice that we are just across from a river—the city's most notorious, filled with the scraps of industry, with unpronounceable compounds and the shed skins of twelve million people, rain washing the rainbow surface of the streets down into the water. We walk to the river's banks and are surprised to find them thickly populated by fit men and women in stretchy outfits and life vests. They are rowers. We see a heat of boats out in the current, testing their speed against the speeds of others.

Under a gray-black bridge, wide enough to make another sky, a sandy slip cuts into the otherwise monolithic bank. A few rowers wade into the water, lift handfuls of it over their shoulders, as on this day it is, indeed, a hot island. It's startling to see human beings swallowed to the thigh by this liquid. We watch them carefully, but they register no immediate harm—no one seems to have cut his foot or burned her skin.

———

Midstream, the rowers' movements are fierce but touchingly simple as they race toward the open sea. We want to think of this day and remember our daring, fill the well. So we take off our shoes, take off the baby's pants. Small waves wash in steadily as if this were a real beach. We hold the baby's hands, walk him into the water and wait for his delight. "Whee," we suggest, studying his face. "Isn't this something?"

As semis and subways pass overhead, our canopy booms and sifts grit into the air. The baby holds tight in a worried joy until we lift him out clean. He comes out cool and clean.

BIRD SPIKES

Our three-year-old says:
Birds would not be very good to play with, would they?
Why?
Because they don't talk like people.
Why else?
Because they're so small. And why else?
Why do you think?
Because they don't have hands.

You can evoke a bird with one, maybe two gestures. One is sufficient—beak or wing, and you're done. Bird.

Yet they are strangers to us. They won't stop moving, won't take a good look at us, they can fly away, we can't cuddle them. We can't even imagine cuddling them, as we cuddle cartoon bears and lions and jaguars.

What do you remember most from visiting Grandpa?
When we poked the dead cormorant with a stick.

Its neck was bent back at an angle we might call "unnatural." What we mean is "untenable," "incompatible with life," because this, too, is natural. We used the stick to stretch the webbing between each toe and leaned close to the lizard skin of the legs and feet. We let the stick test the density of the feathers, felt the light cage of the ribs. The eye was retreating, losing its humours, the beak still hooked and ready to shred. It felt like a gift, being able to get this close. We planned to return each day to track the decay, but we didn't come again.

Where his grandfather lives, the government finds the nests of cormorants and oils their eggs with "food-grade" corn oil. The cormorant parents continue to incubate the eggs while the chicks suffocate inside. Government workers also "cull" adult birds. Cormorants are highly social birds and they mate for life (a trait we admire in geese and swans). Thus one dead cormorant is more than the sum of itself; it equals the death of a breeding pair, the potential dispersal of a flock.

The Department of Natural Resources keeps the cormorants in check to keep the fishing stock up. Cormorants are excellent fishers and excellent breeders, and they can strip lakes of adolescent fish, including the sport fish local and tourist humans—both groups comparatively poor fishers—vie to catch. "Natural Resources," natural resources. The moniker is the grandchild of manifest destiny—that a thing might be both natural and a resource.

With western migration through the U.S. in nineteenth and early twentieth centuries, cormorants' numbers dipped precariously low, settlers ruthless against both threat and abundance. Kill a wolf, collect your bounty; kill a cormorant, a bison, a passenger pigeon, just for fun. After rebounding mid-century, cormorants were thought nearly extirpated in the 1970s, as their food supply filled with pesticides and their eggshells thinned. Environmental groups placed them on watch lists, people built nesting sites. Until the birds did too well.

In our twenty-first century, as people spray corn oil on nests in the north (an oil abundant due to petroleum-based pesticides and fertilizers), others mourn crude oil–soaked wildlife, including cormorants, washing up on the shores of the Gulf of Mexico. *She swallowed the bird to catch the spider... she swallowed the spider to catch the fly, but I don't know why she swallowed the fly. Perhaps she'll die.*

Our boy said, *I want to see pictures of birds. Not real birds, sculptures of birds...cartoon birds.*

We came across this while clicking around on the Internet:

After a couple of strolls through the forest I came up with an idea for a new art-project. I searched the internet to see if such a project already existed or not and.... it didn't (or at least i haven't found the info about it.)

BIRD ART INSTALLATION PROJECT
What's the project about?
* You become a participant (by joining the facebookgroup) and
* make a bird
*hang it in a tree and
*photograph it.

*You place the picture of your bird on the Facebookpage which
is created for this project.
*You and the participating artists from your city/province make
the BIRD ART INSTALLATION from the birds made.
* You document the whole installation (participating artists,
location, how many birds, sizes, materials used, where the birds
in the installation hang and so forth)
* You make photographs/videos of your
BIRD ART INSTALLATION and
* You put the videos on YOUTUBE.

We looked at human-made birds, one after the other—
cute, sincere, mournful, comic, abstract—while the laptop
warmed our legs. What will the next one look like, what
clever idea did someone have, what household materials did
she use? Presently it seemed that these stylized, carefully
positioned, and immobile birds might be the only birds. Or,
at the very least, that they were preferable to the twitching
things we might find outside, who—their hearts racing,
feathers covered in mites—are unwilling to tell us something delightful about ourselves.

We walk him to preschool under a network of scaffolding
and point out messy whorls of grass, feathers, and balloon
strings poking out from around pipes and corrugated metal
roofs. Birds have tucked nests into every available crevice,
used every available material—shred of latex glove, sandwich bag. In the city, scaffolding appears overnight and
usually stays long enough for it to become the new landscape. It comes down without warning, and we may not

recognize the block we've known for years. When it comes down in spring, countless nests and their eggs end up on the sidewalk, until someone sprays the remnants into the street with a hose. We hold him up to see the nests while they're still intact, but he wants his feet on the ground, where he uses them to run at the birds, shouting, startling all but an implacable pigeon into flight.

Oh, don't scare them, we say. How would you feel? But he acts as though he doesn't speak our language.

We recently installed bird spikes on our fourth-floor window ledges to keep pigeons from roosting and destroying our peace with their crooning. We recently gave a time-lapse camera to one of our mothers so she might record the comings and goings at her back-patio bird feeders. We have hung birdhouses, suet, strings of berries. We have cooked sugar water, dropped in red #5 to feed the sporty hummingbirds.

A few blocks from his school is a sign that reads "Forever Wild." It is decorated with a loosely drawn bird—a crane, most likely, given its long neck and legs—and painted brown and cream, colors meant to suggest: we are treading lightly here. It marks a strip of land within a park within this densest of North American urban centers that will remain "without unnecessary intervention" in perpetuity. We are touched by the impossible optimism required by both words: wild, forever.

In Forever Wild, someone has altered a sign to read, "Forever Alone Child." In Forever Wild, someone regularly scatters popcorn around the base of a podium that displays drawings one might use to identify bird species. In Forever Wild, someone leaves kibbles—corn, fats, salt, red #5, and yellow #7 pressed into the gestural shape of tiny fish—in black plastic takeout bowls for feral housecats. We walk through Forever Wild as often as we can.

If birds want us to build them homes, cook and dye sugar water for them, they must remain elusive, perhaps even endangered. If their numbers are robust and they have functional intestines and a penetrating song....

    We got our bird spikes at a home supplies store, but, as it turns out, there are businesses devoted exclusively to bird eradication and extermination.

Bird Solutions International
BirdbGone
Bird Buffer
Bird X
Bird Barrier
Bird Busters
Bird Master
Bird Control, Inc.
Airstrike Bird Control
United Bird Control
All Animal Control
Catch-It Wildlife and Pest Control, Inc.
Avitrol
Nixalite
Flybye

"We solve tough bird problems"
when "nature's beauty is spoiled by pest birds"
and you must make your property "bird hostile."

With bird spikes and sonic cannons
and high volt/low amp electric tracks
and "eagle eye" bird scarers emitting "filtered light beams
in a menacing pattern,"
and, because "birds adapt after exposure to false threats," with
bird wire, bird netting, bird lasers, taste aversion products,
repellent gel, shock strips, live traps followed by "humane ex-
termination," and live raptors provided by "raptor specific
companies" (though the spectacle of raptors shredding pest
birds "might offend some customers").

The summer we poked the dead cormorant with a stick, we
also visited an art installation that allowed visitors to stand
before three separate white screens that mirrored their bodies
in black silhouette.

On the first screen, our fingers broke off into birds and
flew away, then our heads and necks. Our human bodies
dissolved as bird after bird—or were they now ash and cin-
der?—took form and whirled into the white sky.

When we stood in front of the second screen, birds appeared above and began to dive-bomb us, flying away with a
bit of our flesh, such that our bodies shrank to black stumps
and then to nothing, picked apart by a thousand beaks.

In front of the third screen, we lifted an arm and a larger-
than-life wing unfurled with a WHOOSH! And then the
other arm—WHOOSH! We had, at last, the great black

wings of a bird of prey. We stood riveted by ourselves, imperious valkyries. It felt like justice, like destiny. We had passed through something and risen from the nub of our human selves. Wingspan undeniable, nobility apparent from a great distance. We had eaten the heart of our adversary and swelled with its singular power.

Then our turn at the screen was up and we were ushered out the other side. But there was something of the hawk in the way we swiveled our heads toward the next sounds to reach us. Woe betide the sparrow, lark, or finch.

WORK IN PROGRESS

This will be our show:

You walk into a large courtyard filled with trees. A handful of white pine cellphone towers, a host of plastic potted office ficus, inflatable palm trees, trellises thick with vines made of wire, and an assortment of artificial Christmas trees—traditional green, silver, and pink with flocking.

You are not meant to be fooled, thinking for a moment that you have entered a nursery. When you are driving in November past an Indianapolis strip mall advertising a new tanning parlor, you do not think you have seen a living palm tree. When you are assembling the pink tinsel Christmas tree, you are not courting a memory of the sweet, sharp scent of the balsam needles found in your carpet months after. They are new varieties and they do not require what we may not be able to give them—space, history, good air and water.

The cellphone tree, it is stiff no matter the wind. Along the highway, it stands taller than the rest of the trees, as if it used to live in a different forest altogether. The sprigs of needles, like green toilet brushes, barely conceal the transmitters. Birds do not nest, animals cannot climb, woodpeckers would bend their beaks. Only the most inattentive eye, the briefest car-window glimpse could confuse them. We are interested in the eyes of the future—unspecific, unsentimental, unburdened.

The idea is that you get into this forest and you begin to find that your memory of forest is a memory of a memory. You retain a few words—vast, conifer, niche; a few images—mess of branches, shaft of sunlight.

But you may see that you don't need memory at all. You've stepped into an optimistic future: you are no longer certain what came first, the tree or the tower. These trees needed you and your recollection of trees to come into being, but they need you less and less. Less than five minutes ago, more than five minutes from now.

We thought that might be all, boxes and boxes of trees unpacked and assembled, office suppliers and telecommunications companies contacted, cajoled (thank you patrons and taxpayers!). But then we had an idea we rather liked: Well into the courtyard, you will sense something has changed. The trees are not exactly right. It's as if you are scanning the shelves, looking for a favorite product, but the box in your hand is the store brand. The color, the lines, they are so close. But something is off. These trees, the last group you see, they were not made by a machine made by a human. They were made by a human, our best effort at impersonating a machine.

We will use a great deal of plastic to make this piece, and aluminum and epoxy. Nothing with cells—those long, boxy cells we sliced and stained on slides in middle school—or stomata, the tiny mouths on the undersides of leaves. We can't make what we didn't make, but perhaps we can multiply what we have made.

You will notice, we hope you will notice, the care we took with tin foil, with vinyl and a sewing machine, with paint on nylon, which does not like to stick, with the etching of veins and the overgrowth of bark. We have gotten so close to the originals, but you must see in the end that someone has made these. We could not find and pluck all of our hairs from the drying resin.

Yes, we want you to come. We want the physical shapes we have arranged to arrive whole in your mind and stay there, like a survival pack, full of nutrition and fear. The show is for the future, but it opens into the now. We want you to think that we are funny and full and humane. We want you to think: even if the very worst happens, there will probably still be someone who loves me. And by *love* we mean *can give stunningly precise details to a sketch artist*. Your hairline, the contours of the skin between your nose and lip.

We want you to come, of course we do. We want to see your faces, the way they shift out from under themselves. There will be wine. But maybe we are making this for ourselves and the sentiment in our eyes. We do not have to be afraid. We do not have to be afraid. We—the great big we—have the trees we have dreamed of, and they will be more and more. It's not so bad.

AT SEA

A man leans out of an apartment window in a Baltic town and throws into the air a rough model of a cruise ship, half as long as he is. It is possible that he is catching the ship, but this strikes us as unlikely. One would only throw a ship, a train, a car, a plane (imagining oneself as the engine) and not catch them. Unless you mean metaphorically catching a train a plane a ship a bus—luck and self-propulsion equal to a combustion engine; but that luck and that engine are in decline. So—man, open window, cruise ship, and an implied crash. Watching, we get a lift in the belly, then, a few seconds later, we're braced for a sound that will register as either notable or alarming. Splinters on the sidewalk.

Still, we have those few seconds in the air. We suppose we will always have them, because this is a photograph. A photograph used in an advertisement for a gallery show (and, honestly, we don't know if it was taken in a Baltic town, or even if we could name with confidence such a town). We flipped back and back and back in the magazine to the page with the ad—three times and we got blinked into the story of the photograph. We have been walking around under the man and his launched cruise ship for a few days now. The ship is suspended over our heads and we're waiting for it to come down.

But perhaps it won't. We don't know if this tale he's put us in includes gravity. In a tale, we could be turned into something, we could be cooked, we could fall in love at the sight of a shoe, we could die from the most singular, gruesome coincidence, or fail to die from lethal ministrations. We could unzip ourselves from the belly of a beast, or lose our way because the forest, the mountain, the river, the wind are animate and plotting against us. We could sail through the air, on the sea, to the edge of a flat world.

The crash, when we step inside it, is gargantuan and silent and tipped on its side. We're standing on what was once a wall, the former floor to our right, the ceiling to our left. In front of us, mounds of debris, the objects of a great room—a ballroom, a lounge?—at every wrong angle. Everything seems slightly larger than it needs to be, Papa Bear–sized—high-backed barstools, brocade settees, bookshelves still attached to the upended wall, having spilled their books to the splintered mounds below. There is a triangle of books still falling, caught and dangling from the shelves as if this were a photograph come to life. Two flatscreen TVs under rubble still flicker the torsos of newscasters.

At our feet is a wave of orange life vests, so we suppose we're in the inner chamber of a ship. And we suppose, from the royal blue walls, the gilt trim, the piano nailed to the perpendicular floor, that this ship is meant for class-conflicted leisure—scotch and reading lamps during the day, Liszt and Chopin over dinner, and, after, karaoke, cocktail bingo, and midnight chocolate fountains.

Our upright postures are wrong for the room and we find ourselves leaning over, trying to peer into the wreck, to find out what has been wrecked. When upright, we suppose, the room was evidence to its occupants. Evidence that the American rec room and fin-de-siècle European imperialism might be combined, reproduced in the unlikeliest of circumstances, and leased.

When we right ourselves again, we see that books have been gutted and their pages washed up near us—page of *House of Mirth*, page of wasp ecology, page of Hegelian dialectic. No way to turn the page.

And now our eyes have returned to the life preservers and observe two things that needle dread under our skin. One: taped to the back placket of each vest is a flashlight. We imagine a hand stretching up its own back, tugging to release the light in a sideways darkness. And two: the vests show no signs of wear.

There are no bodies. We, on the threshold, are the bodies.

Once upon a time, we are on the sea. Well, we think we are on the sea because we're inside a ship. But we never see the sea, never look outside—we are satisfied in every way with the interior. Our legs and viscera and inner ear register the vast bowl of water upon which we presume we're floating. We are happy to be altered in a way that's beyond our control while never leaving the ship's lounge. We hear that there are many features—a boutique, indoor pool, conference rooms where one might learn to fold paper into a mammal or count to ten in a tonal language, but we find we are happiest just here. We arrive early from our berths, stay late. We've browsed the bookshelves that begin with rows of classics and then give way to mysteries, true crime, and romances, historical and contemporary. There is a well-stocked bar with high-backed chairs, presumably so we might both feel and remain upright while drinking generous cocktails. In this room we dance and read and observe others or pretend to while we gallop after the scrolling ticker at the bottom of the grand televisions. Numbers we cannot decipher dot the borders of the screens. And the ship feeds and feeds us. We spend considerable time imagining what might be brought out next on paper doilies, though we have trouble remembering the last thing we actually tasted.

We're floating on the ocean, we're sure of that. It is, at least, a reasonable guess. But we don't know where, we don't know our captain, we don't know how long we're scheduled to keep up this leisure, these nights with a musical program and a cash bar, the way the staff uses our names so we don't think that they think we are forgettable, expendable.

One night, the room heaves, and we think perhaps this is the beginning of the story. We try to remember the rules of fairy tales: if you see beauty or ugliness, it may be a disguise; proclamations, pleas, and invocations will be repeated three times; and the ending is always known at the beginning. Perhaps one day we'll go up on deck, take in this storied ocean.

But what can we do? We are at sea. We are in a tale. Warnings and predictions go unheeded despite the certainty of their coming true.

FIRST ORDER OF DECAY

Rumors circulated. Interns quit. Depending on who you ask, the gallery was not careful with the wording or it was immaculately precise. Either way, the press release seemed to imply that the upcoming exhibit would be radioactive, with materials hot from Chernobyl. Attendants, they said, would be wearing protective suits; visitors would be asked to sign waivers.

A good deal had been written previously about the artists, mostly by critics, sometimes by journalists on the arts beat, but now they were suddenly, massively famous. Newspapers, morning shows, cable news networks, and blogs frothed over the story, leading with *Has the art world gone too far?* or *Would you risk cancer to see art?* or *While the world reels from Japan's nuclear disaster, one Manhattan art gallery is allegedly bringing radiation to you.* For a day or two, the radioactive exhibit was the dominant topic in online discussion threads and polls: *Environmental art or sensationalism? Should artists who harm the viewer be prosecuted?* A Court TV anchor interviewed a professor of law who said he would be within his rights to attend the gallery show because it might be radioactive and then initiate a lawsuit because it might be radioactive. "We must be protected from our curiosity," he said.

On opening night, it was impossible for most to enter the gallery, impossible even to form a line, the street was so mobbed. News crews jockeyed for position on the pavement; their hot lights and well-drawn telecasters made it seem as if everyone was, indeed, in the right place. A few police units were called in for crowd control. They put barricades on either end of the block and called to one another over their radios: "What's going on here, again? Over." "I don't know. Some stunt. Over." "One of the galleries is supposed to be radioactive. Over." "It's always something. Over." The looks on people's faces were sharp, conspiratorial, sometimes almost greedily amused, as if real things weren't real and their attendance was proof.

The crowds hardly waned after opening night, and reporters returned, hoping in vain for an interview with reluctant gallerists or the artists, who seemed altogether absent. Soon after the opening, though, when officials from Customs and the Nuclear Regulatory Commission began to investigate, the gallerists and their lawyers conceded to interviews. The artist's original intent, they said, was that the materials for the sculptures be salvaged from the forests and deserted towns within the "Zone of Alienation," the ring directly around the Chernobyl power plant meltdown. After all, poachers, loggers, and scavengers regularly smuggled radioactive goods out of the Zone. People could be eating Chernobyl meat or sitting in Chernobyl chairs. But they, the gallerists, would never risk viewers that way. It was all perfectly safe—under pressure, the artists sent materials from the "Chernobyl area," but outside of the restricted zone. Their levels of radiation were acceptable and they'd been legally imported.

After that, the crowds died back enough that one could see the exhibit itself. The walls had been turned into lightboxes and covered in what looked like magnified nature photography—a fuchsia orchid big as a bush, a swallow's oddly folded beak, an animal track in mud, a boar running, nearly in flight. Invisible speakers broadcast layers of birdsong, wolves howling, a sound that might be snuffling in the dirt. Oddly formed trees made of wood scrap, sun-bleached fiberglass, tubing, and rusted metal dotted the cavernous room. It was as if the branches had a hard time knowing which way was up. They grew toward the ceiling, the floor, started toward the ceiling and then shot to the floor. The corners of the room were bubbling with fungi that might have been real or fabricated—people peered closely but couldn't tell.

After the gallerist's statement, it became easy to surmise that these were all images from Chernobyl, from inside the Zone. And because of the exhibit, studies of the Chernobyl area were suddenly given space in the press. They conflicted, as studies will, but some said that while human life had dwindled to a few hundred residents (far fewer than had attended the opening), some flora and fauna had flourished since the meltdown. A national news weekly ran a vivid spread with graphs, photos, and sidebars that showed how rats and mice had mutated greater cell stability, vegetables swelled outrageously, some pine and birch grew as bushes instead of trees, species presumed extinct—bison, lynx, bear, wild horses—thrived in the world's most disconcerting nature preserve. One report said that robots sent into the exploded reactor core returned with a profusion of mushrooms. In a sleight of hand, the accompanying footage pictured button mushrooms growing in manure at a farm upstate. These displays were tantalizing—more arresting, in fact, than the artist's sculptures and photographs. The media reports made the Zone of Alienation seem like both the next hot eco-destination and the old Route 66: gilded with nostalgia for the Cold War era, a place made iconic through abandonment. News outlets made viewers feel many things in quick succession, with grateful amnesia.

There were some easy-to-miss elements of the gallery show, however, that restored the uneasiness the news shorts had chased away. For example, everyone seemed to leave the gallery with dust or ash on her legs. It took a long time to track down the source, but it seemed that movement through the doorway to the exhibit triggered a subtle puff of particles—chalk? The lighting was terrible: fluorescent, overly bright and vibrating here and there from faulty ballasts. People looked waxy and unstable, as if they, themselves, were quivering. Particularly sensitive viewers and those who returned to see the exhibit again noticed a smell in the air, sickly sweet as it persisted. Burnt candy or a chemical sugar. Visitors who lingered also began to feel slightly damp, their hair curling or going limp, their skin clammy. If they looked, they would see numerous tiny nozzles in the ceiling emitting a whisper-fine spray. It was water, distilled water—the gallerists had been pressed to admit in interviews. But people reported feeling ill after leaving, nauseated and irritable. Something with an unknown half-life had crept up on them.

Is this what the artists wanted? The worry, the creep? The conversation turned, in smaller circles now, to whether the artists themselves were sensationalistic, orchestrating a baseless uproar. The timing seemed suspicious—the exhibit going up only months after the second-largest nuclear accident in history. But by all accounts, they had been unreachable except by Ukrainian postbox for four or five years, some claiming they'd been living all that time in the Zone of Alienation. Before this, they seem to have been itinerant, moving every few years, with no permanent studio or home. In the past they'd moved to Prince William Sound after the Exxon Valdez oil spill, to Croatia after the war; they lived on the Bikini atoll and dove the military ship graveyard despite the warnings; they lived on a houseboat in the Pacific, floating in the middle of islands of trash. They sent work from each blighted place.

Some writers called them disaster-mongers, in love with the worst-case scenario. Some said they were like cockroaches or carrion beetles: they came with the microbes, vermin, and reporters after disaster. Some said they were canny, they were sociopaths, they were fueled by their press, exploitative, morbid, nihilist.

But little was known about them—they had never made statements before, had never given interviews, didn't allow books to be made of their catalogue, didn't give talks or authorize pictures of themselves. Perhaps this, too, was calculated, the "greater press through no press" strategy. Except their self-imposed isolation was thorough and committed. True narcissists would have starved under such stringency.

Others said they are the future in the present, that is, psychologically, biologically. We watch them to know what's coming our way—how to see, how to make a home in all those places that don't seem to want us, because of something we've done.

The last known place they'd been before the Zone of Alienation was New Orleans. Not long after Hurricane Katrina retreated, they bought three adjacent lots in the Ninth Ward for almost nothing and spent more than a year camped on one while they attempted to build the other two up to sea level. They carted mud and sand and piles of sea sediment to the lots in industrial food buckets and then with a found wheelbarrow. They posted pictures of each load—hundreds of remarkably similar photographs.

When this did not move fast enough and the soil threatened to simply slide into neighboring lots, they erected scrap-wood scaffolding around the mounds and began tossing debris from the flood down onto them. A sign in front said "Flood Fill Wanted," and, daily, people backed up onto the property and tossed out couch cushions, collapsed chairs, boxes of swollen books, file cabinets with broken locks, car seats, and endless black plastic bags, mystery bags no one opened.

From blocks away, one could smell the dankness. Even atheists say the smell post flood is the smell of evil. And the artists lived next to the smell for a year. But it seems like that was what they wanted—to test their senses, their stamina and sanity. To get down with what happens next. Right there in it, nostrils full.

The tower became a landmark, the highest point for many acres. Some said it was more blight, an eyesore; some considered it a monument; some said at least all that crap is gathered up in one place; some said now we'll have something to hold onto when the waters breach again— they are *going* to breach again. One critic considered the yearlong project as performance art, but then said such art was bankrupt. The energy they spent on this tower could have gone to building new homes or schools. People were hurting, the critics said, and a tower of ugliness sharpened the sting.

They disappeared one day, their tents disassembled in the night and wedged into the sculpture through gaps in the scaffolding. Had they finished? And what did finished mean? Public record shows they still own the deeds, but they left nothing else behind—no sign, no press release, no other evidence of their presence besides the paths they'd worn in the ground.

Records also show that the city occasionally issues fines for property dereliction and fines for non-payment of fines. But to have torn down their sea-level tower would have taken more money than the city had or cared to spend on the Ninth.

A few years ago, the tower turned into a pyre, and accounts made their way into local papers, post-Katrina blogs, and photo streams. At least one headline said, "Well-known artists' work destroyed by fire." It was kids, some said, teenagers looking for something big to feel in the moment and to talk about after. Maybe it was a community action—people tired of what they saw as a pile of trash. A rumor circulated in the art world that the artists themselves had returned to light it up. The fire department brought a truck down and watched the tower burn. A crowd gathered, of course, flames still calling to something deep down. But it was safe this night, a peaceful buzzing. People brought folding chairs and bags of chips and watched the flames and the water like it was television. On account of the heat, jacked up by the burning tower, the fire truck turned one hose into a giant fountain. Neighbors dashed up to it, shrieking; kids rode dirt bikes and scooters through it, performing tricks for the crowd. On that night, it didn't matter who was artist and who was spectator.

After the fire, there had been silence about the artists for years until what became known as the Chernobyl show. Now, a recent article in a Manhattan arts and leisure magazine—entitled "Ghost Hunting in the Art World," about artists who remained eccentrically reclusive or elusive—claimed that all inquiries sent to their Ukrainian postbox were met with a stark white postcard bearing an invitation to visit them in the Zone of Alienation. New work would be discussed, statements given, and questions answered only there. If interested, contact them again with dates for the visit, and they will respond with GPS coordinates.

The biggest surprise is how cheerful they are. And easy in their skins. They had seen occasional adventurers, natives, and poachers over the years, but until now no one who had been looking for them had taken them up on their offer of a visit. The paperwork involved, particularly with a child, was not negligible; we were scrutinized in ways mysterious and apparent to us for months. We could imagine either everything or nothing in our past presenting itself as evidence; what we couldn't see was a specific pattern in our personal data, stories that distinguished us from cohorts. And, in fact, authorities with stationery and stamp pads, authorities we would never meet, let us slip through, three bodies entering into a distinct temporal dimension, seemingly pre- and post-human all at once.

The artists live in a cottage on what used to be farmland around the village Opachichi. Now it's mostly a birch and pine forest, but they've re-cultivated a handful of acres. The area directly around the cottage is dotted with the ramshackle outbuildings of homesteaders: a lean-to woodshed, henhouse, well, smoke shack for preserving fish and game, drying shed, outhouse, and solar shower. A small orchard near the cottage has withstood fallout and neglect and looks to bear apples, pears, and plums. No fanciful touches, no totems that would announce them as artists. Except perhaps two bushes that flank the cottage door, which on second look aren't bushes at all but birch trees grown short and round. The artists are all smiles, delighted to give a tour; they offer a lunch of fresh eggs, asparagus, bread, and preserves. The bread, they say with chagrin, is Ukrainian government rations; they didn't have time to make a fresh loaf. After lunch, there is homemade raspberry liqueur. The child is desperate for someone to animate a sock or a scarf or a stuffed bird so that he might have a serious conversation about the professions he intends to hold. After he falls asleep on the musty settee, the camaraderie of country isolation fades and the questions begin:

Do you think it's safe, living here, drinking the water, eating the animals or growing vegetables in the soil?

Safe? It's safe in the sense that we know it's unsafe.

Why do you make people come to you? It would be easy for you to stay here but still communicate with people around the world, to send writing and pictures. You could send more work to a gallery.

Well, we think there's something to be gained from crossing the border into the Zone of Alienation. Over the border, the roads become weedy, more like just the suggestion of roads; towns look like either old movie sets or slag heaps; signs seem engineered for nostalgia. But you've never heard anything like dusk here. The air, it almost seems to vibrate—there are thousands of birds looking to roost and insects in a frenzy, maybe on their last night. And then the wolves start calling. People only want to talk about the meltdown, the human accident. But that sound is a beautiful accident, one of a hundred thousand accidents down the line.

But you want other people to risk their health? I mean, here we are...

The only thing that stops or pauses at the border is humans. Birds don't pause. Animals don't. Water, wind, soil, pollen, seeds, bugs don't pause at the border.

How long do you plan on staying here?
This is it. We won't leave now—we're home.

You know, you make some people very angry. They say you court death, moving to the most toxic disaster areas in the world. That you're driven by hubris or self-regard—you think you're impervious, or that your art is so important that it's worth the risk. They think you're profligate with your health, and, you know, it deeply offends them. They say you probably haven't experienced real pain or illness in your life and don't understand how pain might deform your minds and not just your bodies. It's not like a philosophy means much when your bones are turning to chalk.

Well. Well. It's no small thing to hear this criticism. One feels, of course, the sting of being misunderstood. We're not sentimental about our lives, it's true. But it took a long time to burn away that sentiment. For many years, our minds were relentlessly occupied with images of cell mutation and cell function disruption and unchecked cell growth, unchecked cell death. Grandparents, an aunt, a parent died of it. We held in our mind's eye side-by-side pictures of healthy and diseased organs, healthy and dented eggs, healthy and paralyzed sperm. Imagine, to name just one example, the masses of prescription drugs flushed through urine streams, then sewage systems, then elsewhere—every pill, every day, every drop going somewhere. And we are that somewhere. We couldn't pretend that with enough money, a high enough gate, or virtuous enough living, we might escape.

It was an instinct long ago, one we didn't even name, that told us not to wait in fear for the seepage to crawl up our hem, not to consider ourselves healthy until someone told us we were sick. A ten-day-old fetus has heavy metals in its stem cells. We didn't wait and order herbs over the Internet or visualize healthy white cells or wear masks on heavy smog days or petition governments or purchase plush toys from wildlife nonprofits. We assumed we were sick and that "cure" was an anachronistic term. We went to the worst of it; we wanted to understand what the future might look like, even if we wouldn't be part of it.

Are you environmental extremists?

But what does environment mean? What is extreme? Oceans within oceans that can't support life? A half-life of 244,000 years? We've cast our lot with acceptance and followed it all the way through.

Do you still have emotions? Or have you "evolved past" them?

Here is a map of the Earth. Look at this—it shows every area that is either anaerobic, perpetually burning, or irradiated. We have a lot of emotions about this map and its color coding. If you stayed for a few weeks, you might be able to record them all. But here, taste the raspberry pulp in this—here, here's an emotion. We push the berries through cheesecloth and our fingers smell of it for hours after.

Are you working on a show now?

We're working on a will. It specifies our final show—we'd like our organs to be displayed—both "healthy" and "diseased"—for as long as will be allowed. And microscopes will be available throughout the room with slides of growths. We're debating about placing magnified pictures of the cells on the walls. Most of all, we would like the visitor to be able to touch the organs and tumors, really get intimate with the insides of a human body. But we doubt this will be allowed.

Why did you become artists?

We started making art because we could no longer speak to our childhood selves. Childhood was lush gardens, tubs of clay, fairy tales read on porch swings, puddles teeming with life, and drawings of animals that no longer exist or won't in another fifty years. We loved those children, we love them still. But they were like characters in a book from another century, and they were so lost in this, the actual world.

Did you ever imagine having children yourselves? (We glance together at the boy. His eyelids are closed and smooth, the eye sockets strikingly round, his mouth ajar and leaking saliva.)

Factories have children, earthquakes have children, plastics have children, jellyfish have children, nuclear reactors have children. We have enough children.

Why aren't you afraid?

We are afraid. We're not afraid because it's so busy here without us.

What if we can't help but be afraid?

YEAR 0

We have been studying maps of projected sea levels for years: a decade from now, two decades, five. We will lose, eventually, the coasts. We must change, eventually, our ways. Prepare our infrastructure, retreat to higher ground.

Then comes the one-hundred-year flood. The hurricane that sweeps anything unbolted across the city's grid. We fill a few extra bottles of water, fill the tub and watch debris accumulate on its surface, make a trip to the store for milk and oats and chocolate. We feel our building sway in the night, hear it groan, as if we live in a tree house. But it stands and the streets around us are not coursing. We try not to cry when, in the park of our son's babyhood, we pick our way around the uprooted cherry trees. Half the city is dark, the outer boroughs drowned.

The galleries have gone under, sandbags and electrical tape insufficient against the surge. Current shows and storerooms, private collections, saturated beyond salvage. The dumpsters fill with pulped walls and prints and sculpture. Paper records are literally frozen to arrest the damage. An irony: in anticipation of the flood, the gallery with the wrecked cruise ship moves it board by cracked board, life preserver by unused life preserver, to an upper floor, where it is untouched.

———

Our child has taken to frequent beheadings. We worried at first: Whither the softness of the baby, the toddler? But now we hack and slash and pierce with gusto. We make, from foam and wood and knotted cloth, the battle gear of the ancient Greek, the Hittite, the samurai, and then give each other what for until the fatal blow: a sword through the heart, or a severed head.

Someone once suggested we were nihilistic. We balked—is it nihilistic to try to wean ourselves from the cycle of hope and despair? To try to enter the stream of time that has no particular interest in our species?

We are hopeful, still. For what, we aren't sure. That we will all rise from the next battle with our limbs and necks restored. That, as our friend says, "Life loves mud."

The floodwaters came. They have come. They will come again, higher next time. Longer. There will be new coasts, another battle, more mud.

ACKNOWLEDGMENTS

Thanks to Nancy Mayer, brilliant reader, most trusted compass, constitutional home. Thanks to Tali Hinkis for her future mind and the LoVid family for, more often than not, being our "we." Thanks to Ashley Byler and family for being our second family. Thanks to Wendy S. Walters for years of inspiration, challenge, and friendship. Thanks to Dale Megan Healey for company in loss and delight in shared interests. Thanks to Stacy Parker LeMelle and Melody Nixon for collaboration, co-curation, and friendship (and to Stacy for last lines). Thanks to Stacey D'Erasmo for fantastic adventure and modeling just about everything I hope to learn. Thanks to Jon Kessler and Sam Lipsyte for greatness of spirit and the right words at the right time. Thanks to Ted Conover for continued support. Thanks to Hannelore Repetto for her support and humor. Thanks to Alice Sohn. Thanks to Dzanc Books, particularly Michelle Dotter, for support of the manuscript and great insight in its journey to becoming a book. Thanks to Katie Shima for her fathomless drawings. Thanks to John Berger for the marks of every sort he left behind. Thanks to the many artists and writers who have altered my neural pathways. Thanks to Douglas and Beals Repetto, supreme neural pathway alterers, beloved creatures, and my perpetual first person plural. And always, always love and gratitude to my mother for everything. She had all the good stuff.

I'm tremendously grateful to the following journals for previously publishing essays and stories that appear in this book.

AGNI
Black Warrior Review
BOMB Magazine
Boston Review
The Collagist
Denver Quarterly
diagram
elimae
Everyday Genius
Gettysburg Review
Hobart
Hotel Amerika
Kenyon Review
New England Review
PANK
Pleiades
Salt Hill Review
Seneca Review
Triquarterly Review